Faith Shapers

Kids' club resources for eight to eleven year olds

Nadia Herbert

Scripture Union

Faithshapers
25 crafts with a message for kids groups

Scripture Union books are published in Australia by

Scripture Union Resources for Ministry Unit
Locked Bag 2
Central Coast Business Centre
NSW 2252
Australia
www.scriptureunion.org.au

and in the United Kingdom by
Scripture Union
207-209 Queensway
Bletchley, MK2 2 EB
England
www.scriptureunion.org.uk

The National Library of Australia Cataloguing-in-Publication entry

Herbert, Nadia.
Faith shapers : 25 crafts with a message for children aged
8 to 11 years.

For Christian leaders of children 8 to 11 years.
ISBN 1 876794 36 4.

1. Christian education of children. 2. Children -
Religious life. I. Title.

268.432

Managing Behaviour in Kids' Groups on page 49 is adapted from an article written by
Deborah Wagner for *KidsWise* magazine © Scripture Union

DTP and cover design by Communique Graphics, Mount Waverely, Victoria, Australia.

Printed by Openbook Print
0532-04

Faith-Shaping PROGRAMMES

The Bible is full of life-giving messages that can transform children and set them on a life-long adventure with God. But effectively communicating these messages to children can be a challenge, right?

Children aged eight to eleven are *not* characterised by a desire to sit still and listen.

They love to

EXPLORE TALK MAKE DO

INTERACT WITH THE WORLD AROUND THEM

That's how most children learn best.

Each of these 25 programmes revolves around a practical, hands-on craft activity, something children can get creatively involved with, something worth taking home. For the leader, there are clear, step-by-step instructions to follow, along with a materials list and an indication of the time needed to complete the craft.

But better than that, each craft is linked to a theme designed to help children grow in faith. There's a relevant Bible verse, a simple prayer, and a catchy Bible message, with short, sharp ways of presenting each.

And that's the core of your programme. Simple.

Most of the teaching is informal, but it's very focused and intentional. A few well chosen sentences (which this book gives you in bold), some ideas to think about and discuss, and lots of activity, make each programme a winner with both leaders and children.

ENJOY!

Good CHOICE!

All the crafts in this book are made from materials that are easy to obtain and inexpensive. They have been designed keeping in mind busy volunteer leaders and the limitations of a church budget. While most of these materials are available from large discount warehouses or chain stores it's also worth browsing your local craft shops and recycling centres to see what's there that could add interest and sparkle to these projects.

There are many wonderful mediums through which children can express their creative side and explore faith in a group setting.

DISPLAY DOUGH RECIPE

Ingredients
(sufficient for a group of about ten children)

- 10 cups plain white flour
- 5 cups salt
- 4.5 cups water

Mix the flour and salt evenly. Add the water gradually to produce a soft, pliable consistency. Mix in a food processor or in a large bowl with a wooden spoon.

Store in a cold place in an airtight container.

Air-drying clay, sometimes called self-hardening clay, is available in small and large packs. It takes twenty-four hours to dry at room temperature and leftover clay can be stored indefinitely in cling wrap in a cool place.

Display dough can be made at home from the recipe on this page. It keeps for one week in the fridge in an airtight container. All dough crafts **must** be varnished after modelling to repel moisture.

Felt can be purchased on the roll from large craft and fabric stores. Precut it yourself to the approximate size required and show children how to cut what they need from the edge of a piece to minimise wastage.

Think about cleanup of both the children and the area they'll meet in. Prevention is invariably better than cure when it comes to paint on furniture and stains on clothes.

A list of requirements is given for each individual craft, but other useful items to have on hand are

- Clean jars or ice cream containers for washing brushes during painting activities
- A good supply of old newspapers and paper towels
- Rags for clean up and spills
- Plastic sheeting (available from hardware stores) to protect desks/tables
- Aprons/art shirts or other protective clothing
- A pair of left-handed scissors

TAKE CARE!

The care of children involves more than making sure they don't cut their fingers or burn themselves. The goal should be to ensure the safety and wellbeing of all children at all times during your programme.

- Affirm the child's worth, dignity and significance in the ways you speak and relate.
- Avoid favouritism and attitudes that 'put down' children. Make every attempt to love and care even for those who are not so easy to love.
- Avoid close physical contact unless in exceptional circumstances such as giving medical attention or for the protection of a child from harm. Learn appropriate ways to sensitively disconnect from over-affectionate children.
- Remain in sight of other people in one-to-one situations with a child.
- Be sensitive to the cultural and family backgrounds of children. This may affect the level of participation of children in activities. Avoid making statements about other religions, cultures or family settings that reflect ignorance, bias or ridicule.
- Do not exploit gender, physical or intellectual differences. Give positive messages.

In addition here are some very practical common sense precautions that that need to be taken to ensure physical safety.

- Ensure a child/adult ratio appropriate for the activity.
- Don't allow children to run around in a crowded room.
- Wipe up spills immediately, particularly on the floor.
- Discourage children from putting anything into their mouth.
- Use non-toxic, washable marker pens and paints.
- Ensure adequate ventilation when using varnishes and glues that smell.
- Always supervise the use of spray cans.
- Make sure any of your own equipment that is unsuitable for children is out of sight.
- Closely supervise the use of anything sharp like craft knives and skewers.

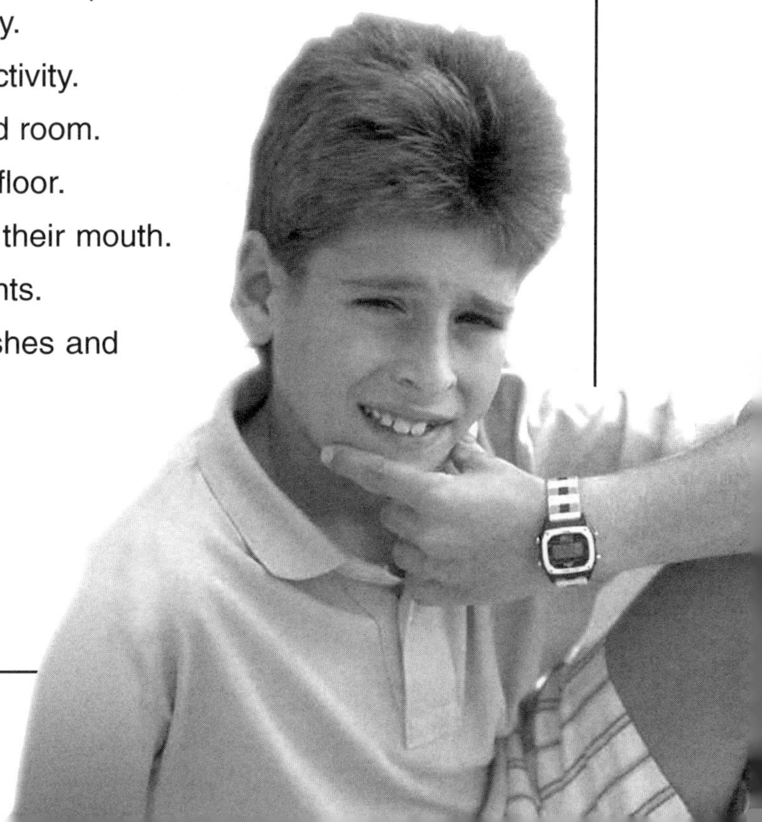

Projects & PROGRAMMES

1

Making a banner encourages the children to think about God and their relationship with him.

Bible reading

John 1:12,13 *... some people accepted him and put their faith in him. So he gave them the right to be the children of God. They were not God's children by nature or because of any human desires. God himself was the one who made them his children.*

You will need

- hemmed calico 150 cm by 50 cm for each child
- acrylic paints (assorted colours)
- paintbrushes

Time required

45 minutes

Message

We can be part of God's family, getting to know him better all the time.

With the group

1. Choose a volunteer to read the Bible verses aloud.
2. **We are all special to God, every one of us. God loves our different personalities. When people choose to believe in God and want to know him through prayer, worship and reading the Bible, God welcomes those people into his family.**
3. Say the message aloud, then invite the children to say it with you.
4. **The banners we'll make can reflect who we are. The aim is to include things on your banner that make you different from everyone else – your talents, interests, looks and personality. For example, a picture of you playing sport could show how important sport is to you; a cut-out book could show that you enjoy reading; a sketch of your favourite pet could show a love of animals. Think about yourself and God too. See if you can include something on your banner that shows what it's like between you and God.**
5. Give out the hemmed calico, acrylic paints and paintbrushes. It may be convenient and practical for the children to work on the floor. Challenge them to express their individuality in creative and different ways, perhaps including their handprint, name and the date.
6. When the children have completed their banners, ask for a volunteer to read the prayer to the group.

I'm Special!

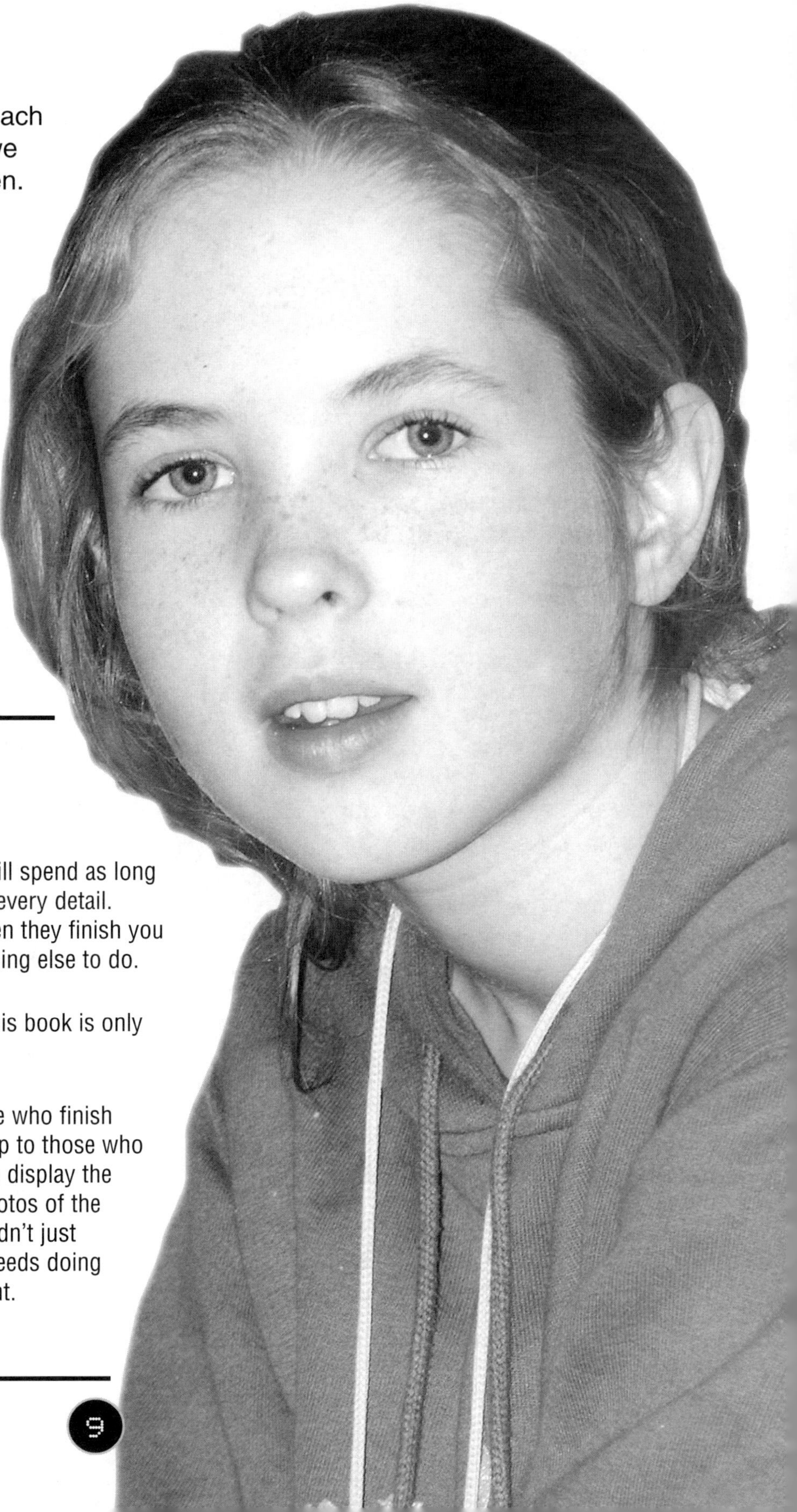

Prayer

Father God, we know you love us and each of us is special to you. Thank you that we can get to know you and be your children. Amen.

Do it differently!

1. Use large sheets of card, paints, and textured fabric, instead of calico.
2. Join the individual banners together to display in the church or the meeting room.

Think Ahead

Children do things at different rates. Some will spend as long as possible on a project, slowly attending to every detail. Others just can't wait to be finished. And when they finish you can be sure that they'll be looking for something else to do.

The time required listed for each activity in this book is only a guide.

So, have interesting tasks to suggest to those who finish ahead of the others. It may involve giving help to those who would welcome it, or getting ready an area to display the finished items, or making signs, or taking photos of the others working. Whatever you suggest shouldn't just keep them occupied but be something that needs doing and will give them a sense of accomplishment.

2

This personal prayer book can encourage children to keep in touch with God.

Bible reading

Matthew 6:9-13 *You should pray like this:*
Our Father in heaven,
help us to honour your name.
Come and set up your kingdom,
so that everyone on earth will obey you,
as you are obeyed in heaven.
Give us our food for today.
Forgive us for doing wrong,
as we forgive others.
Keep us from being tempted
and protect us from evil.

You will need

- one piece of shiny gold card 22 cm by 15 cm for each child
- twelve pieces of coloured paper 22 cm by 15 cm for each child
- scissors
- hole punch (two holes)
- chord, ribbon or wool, 20 cm for each child
- pens
- coloured marker pens
- craft scissors (to cut decorative edges)

Time required

40 minutes

Message

By praying regularly, we grow closer to God.

With your group

1. Display the words of the Lord's Prayer and show where they occur in the Bible. Challenge the group to be able to say them with you by the end of the lesson.

2. **Who has trouble knowing what to say when they pray? Jesus used the Lord's Prayer to teach his disciples what to say. Praying helps us grow closer to God. It sometimes helps to write down things we pray for – things that we know God would want to do for us and for others. Having our own 'prayer book' can help us pray more. As well as listing the things you talk with God about, you could use it as a journal and write in it things you think God is communicating to you as you pray.**

3. Say the message aloud and invite the children to say it back to you.

4. Hand out the gold card, coloured paper, hole punch, scissors and chord. Show the children how to use the coloured paper as pages, and the gold card as a cover for their prayer book. Have them carefully align the cover and the pages and then use the hole punch on the left side to make two holes. Some children may need help with this. Give each child some chord to thread through the holes to secure the cover and pages together. Knot the chord firmly on the top of the cover to complete the 'prayer book'. Decorate the cover and the pages with craft scissors and coloured markers.

Time to Pray

5. **The Lord's Prayer is like a model that we can use when we pray.**
   Invite the children to copy the Lord's Prayer onto the first page of their decorated book. Suggest that they choose a fixed time to pray every day, such as at bedtime, or 'wake up' time.

6. Allow the children time to write down any prayer requests they have, then suggest they look through the book of Psalms and choose some prayers from the Psalms that might help them as they pray.

7. Conclude by inviting the children to share how they think they'll use their books and then say the Lord's Prayer together.

Chat as you go

As the children make their prayer books, discuss some of the following aspects of prayer.

- God listens to our spoken prayers and hears our silent ones too.
- When we pray, it is like talking directly to him.
- We can be totally honest when we pray.
- God always listens and answers his people wisely.
- Prayer isn't for us to get what we want; it's for us and others to get what's good and right - what God wants. We must not be selfish or greedy when we pray.

Tap into the children's experiences and challenge them to discover more about prayer by praying more.

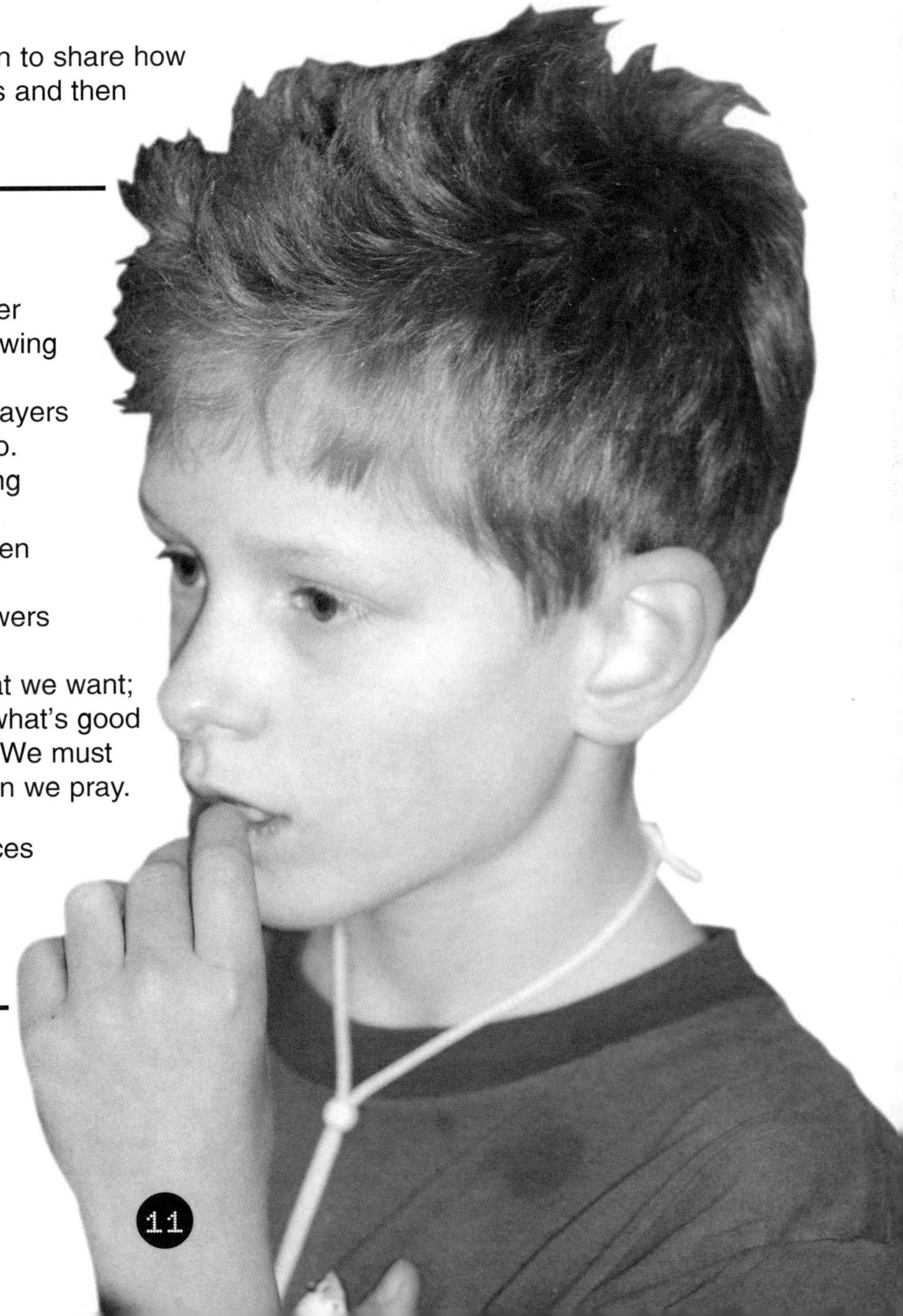

Clay is wonderful for expressing creativity. This sculpting activity can help chilren to understand how valuable they are to God.

Bible reading

Psalm 139:1,2 *You have looked deep into my heart, Lord, and you know all about me. You know when I am resting or when I am working, and from heaven you discover my thoughts.*

1 Samuel 16:7 *People judge others by what they look like, but I judge people by what is in their hearts.*

You will need

- air-drying clay
- modelling tools (or plastic knives)
- acrylic paints (assorted colours)
- paintbrushes (selection of sizes)
- rolling pins

Time required

35 minutes

Message

God loves me just as I am.

With your group

1. Write the message on the whiteboard. When the children come in, encourage them say it aloud to each other in different voices. To help them visualise the words, rub out the message and play a speedy game in which you ask how many times each letter occurs in the message, with everyone calling out the answer.

2. **God does not judge us by our looks, or our weaknesses. He understands who we are and loves every one us. God made us with different personalities, appearances, talents and abilities. To God, we are all important and valuable.**

3. Choose volunteers to read the Bible verses to the group.

4. Give everyone a piece of clay the size of a tennis ball, a rolling pin, and modelling tools/plastic knives to make a head and shoulders clay sculpture of themselves.

5. Distribute the paints and paintbrushes for the children to paint their sculptures. (Allow about 10 minutes.)
   Note: The sculptures will take 24 hours to dry at room temperature.

6. Conclude by asking for a volunteer to read the prayer.

TIP

The easiest way to make the sculpture is to roll the clay 2 cm thick, cut out the shape of a head, neck and shoulders, then use the remaining clay to make hair and features. Alternatively, the children can make a three-dimensional head and shoulders, then mould the features. (Allow about 20 minutes.)

Let's face it

Prayer

Dear God, we know you see us from heaven.
We want you to be pleased with us.
Help us to be faithful to you.
Amen.

THINK AHEAD

Praying with your group

You can't *make* anyone pray.

Sometimes it's best not to try.

Having said that, prayer is such a vital part of relating to God that we should be doing our utmost to encourage children to experience prayer for themselves.

Prayer develops the relationship between the God of the universe and his people. Children are full of energy and preoccupied with the things around them. Praying with children is about connecting them and their world to God.

Your starting point in praying with children will differ according to the context. Are the children used to praying alone/aloud/at home/in a school setting?

Don't assume that they are used to praying or feel comfortable praying aloud. Don't assume that they are not, either. Helping children pray is a process.

Be sensitive. Children may come from different Christian traditions, other faith communities or from homes where there is no prayer. Be aware of those who don't feel they have a relationship with God.

4

Make this keepsake jar as a reminder of the gifts God gives.

Bible reading

James 1:17 *Every good and perfect gift comes down from the Father who created all the lights in the heavens. He is always the same and never makes dark shadows by changing.*

You will need

- one small clean jar with lid for each child
- dried leaves
- feathers
- shells
- dried flower heads
- gold foil
- pictures cut from magazines of homes, pets, people laughing ...
- acrylic paints (assorted colours)
- paintbrushes
- plasticine

TIP

Before the session, remove labels from the jars and cover any writing on the lid with paint or contact.

Time required

40 minutes

Message

God gives us good gifts because he loves us.

With your group

1. Read the Bible verse to the children or play a game to reveal the words. (See page 55).
2. **We know that God loves us because of the good things he gives us. What are some of them?** Write suggestions on the whiteboard. Encourage them to think of less tangible things like relationships, surprises, memories, God's forgiveness and his Spirit with us.
3. Read the message aloud, then invite the children to say it with you, perhaps writing it on their jar.
4. Spread out the materials so the children have easy access to them. Explain that a keepsake jar can be a reminder of God's good gifts to us. Discuss some things that could go in their jars, such as shells to remember a happy vacation at the beach; feathers representing beautiful birds, pictures of people for families and friendship, gold foil for sunlight. A sketch or diagram could be a reminder of a time when they especially felt God's presence.

   Encourage them to think creatively about God's gifts before filling their jars. Challenge them to think symbolically, choosing what's available or modelling something with the plasticine to represent something they can't possibly put in their jar, like a screwed up ball of paper to represent a tree or a bottle top to represent a cool drink on a hot day. Create a fun atmosphere encouraging guessing competitions around what goes in the jar.
5. Suggest that they paint one of God's gifts on the lid or sides of the jar.

God's gifts

6. Put the jars aside to dry. Encourage them to keep their jars at home and add to them as they think of something appropriate.
7. Ask everyone to think of one thing that they are thankful for and incorporate it into the prayer. Alternatively allow a minute for everyone to hold their jars and reflect on the good things God has given them, silently telling God how they feel.

Prayer

Heavenly Father, we are thankful for the wonderful gifts you give us, our families, friends, church and school. We specially say thank you for ... (let volunteers add their own idea). Amen.

Make it better – for some

Don't be surprised if some of your group rate spiders and insects among God's best gifts. Steer clear of anything dangerous and actively discourage cruelty to living things but be prepared to stretch your admiration to what interests the children.

THINK AHEAD

Praying with your group

(continued...)

If children in your group are unfamiliar with the concept of prayer, explain that prayer is simply communicating with God. Talk with them about what they know about God. Some children's image of God may be such that they want to avoid communicating with him. If that's the case, over time share what you've experienced of God's love and acceptance.

Make it an aim to model prayer in a variety of situations. Be very brief and specific when praying with a group of children. Go into it naturally without waiting for total stillness or silence. Avoid jargon. Use appropriate language that children will understand. Be relevant. Pray for matters that arise in conversation. Be natural. Use conversational tone and language.

Provide opportunities for children to pray silently or aloud, if they choose.

These programmes have a prayer included because reading a prayer that someone else has written can be a good start for children who have no idea what to say. But encourage them to form their own prayers, starting perhaps by adding a word or phrase to someone else's prayer.

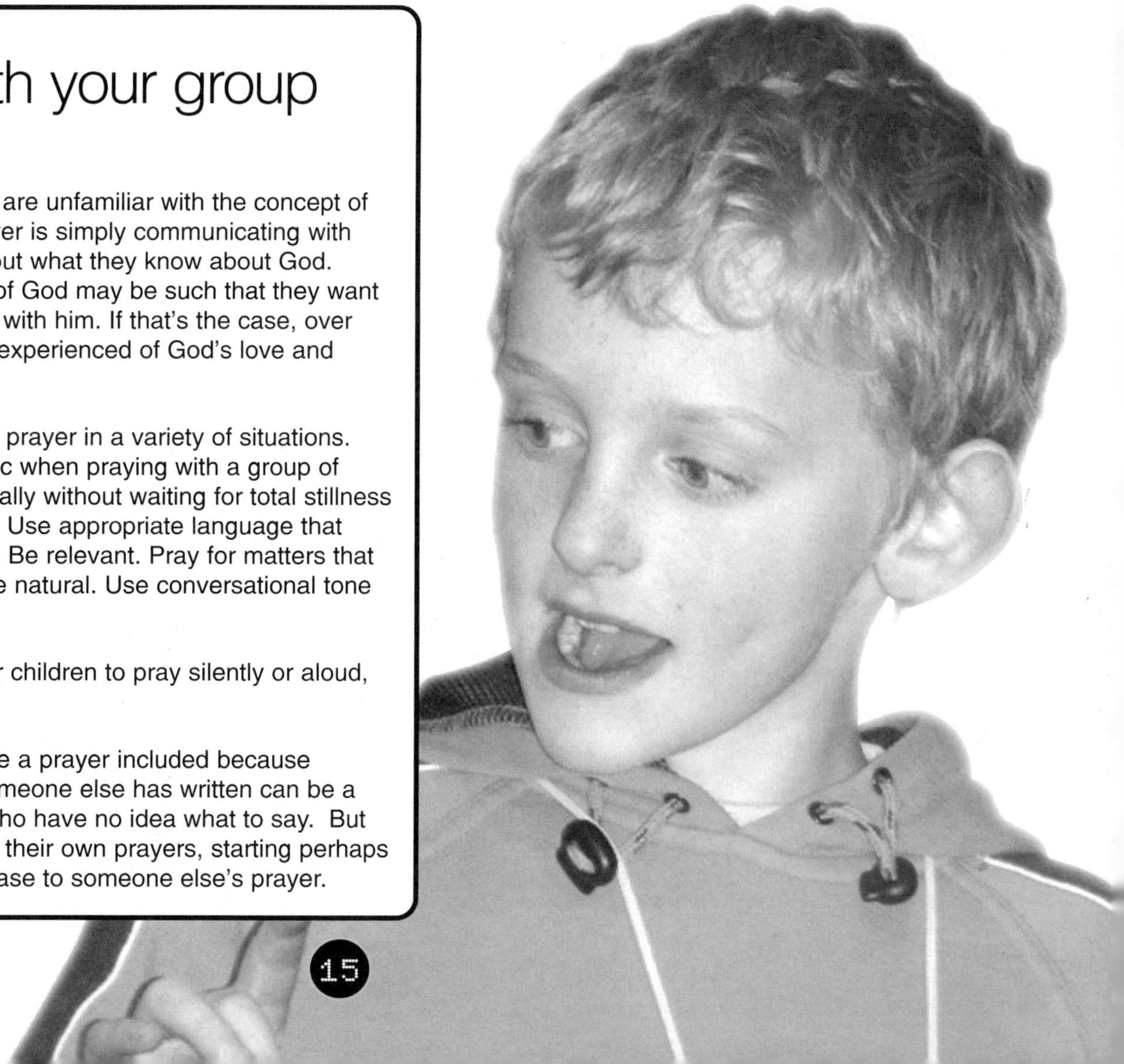

5

Children will enjoy making this medal from display dough as they think about serving God.

Bible readings

Philippians 3:14 *I run toward the goal, so that I can win the prize of being called to heaven. This is the prize that God offers because of what Christ Jesus has done.*

2 Timothy 4:7,8 *I have fought well. I have finished the race, and I have been faithful. So a crown will be given to me for pleasing the Lord. He judges fairly, and on the day of judgment he will give a crown to me and to everyone else who wants him to appear with power.*

You will need

- display dough made from the recipe on page 4
- wooden skewers
- rolling pins
- round cookie or scone cutters
- gold acrylic paint
- paintbrushes
- baking trays
- baking parchment
- one 90 cm piece of narrow white ribbon for each child
- folk art varnish or clear wood varnish (gloss)

Time required

40 minutes

Message

We can make it our goal to do our best for God.

With your group

1. Read one or more of the Bible verses aloud to the children.

2. **People who believe in Jesus try to do their best for him. Living for Jesus is as challenging as it is for an athlete running a race. There's a prize when we finish running the race of life. The prize is life in heaven with God. We're going to make an Olympic-style winner's medal to represent our prize for leading a life that pleases God**

3. Say the message aloud, then encourage the children to say it with you.

4. Distribute the display dough (a lump the size o a walnut should be sufficient), rolling pins and cutters. Have the children roll their dough out evenly 1 cm thick, then press the cookie cutter firmly into the dough to make the medal. Discard the excess dough. Show the children how to smooth the edges of the medal using their fingers.

5. Hand out the wooden skewers, gold paint and paintbrushes. Using the skewers, the children will need to make a hole near the top of their medals to thread with ribbon after baking. The hole needs to be 0.5 cm wide so it is still open when baked.

6. Paint the medals with gold paint, then carve a number "1" in the centre with the skewer. Add second coat of gold paint, then carefully place the medals on baking trays lined with baking parchment. Make sure you have a foolproof way of identifying each medal with its maker.

   The medals will need to be baked for nine hours at 120 °C/gas mark 0.5. Varnish both sides and then thread with ribbon when the varnish has dried.

first prize

7. Choose a volunteer to read the prayer to the group. Alternatively, encourage children who are comfortable praying aloud to share things about living for God that they find difficult and then pray for each other.

Prayer

Our Father in heaven, please help us to serve you faithfully and always do our best for you. Amen.

Make it better

Raid your kitchen utensils drawer and give children the opportunity of personalising their medals by pressing interesting shapes carefully around the edge. Forks, serrated knives (blunt ones), and peelers work well. So do tools from modelling clay sets. A plastic number one from a puzzle or magnetic number set can be used for marking the centre of the medal.

Joining children on the spiritual journey

Many in children's ministry have their hands full just keeping the children occupied and out of mischief during their programs. They focus on good relationships and making sure everyone has a good time so they keep coming back. But they find that trying to convince active kids to listen to a five minute talk on some aspect of the Christian faith is about all the spiritual input that's possible. They hope that something that's seen or heard will somehow take root and later bear fruit.

On the other hand some leaders have found that spiritual things fascinate children. While they often find knowledge *about* Christianity unappealing, children are very keen to hear about God at work in an other person's life. In fact, even the ones with no connection to any church, often have 'God moments' in their own life that they struggle to make sense of if they don't hear others talk about such things. To explore this further *Children and the Gospel* by Ron Buckland (Scripture Union 2001) is a good resource.

If you usually think of the children in your group as 'blanks' with little or no knowledge or experience of God, consider how to relate to them as people in whom God is already at work, drawing them to himself. Think of the children as being on a spiritual journey and work out ways of nurturing any faith that it within them. Pray for them as you prepare your sessions, but make it your goal to pray *with* them as well. You may be the only person who does.

6

Designing and decorating this T-shirt will promote thinking and discussion about following Jesus.

Bible reading

John 8:12 (*Jesus*) *said, 'I am the light for the world! Follow me, and you won't be walking in the dark. You will have the light that gives life.'*

You will need

- a plain white (or light coloured) T- shirt for each child
- T-shirt markers (available from large chain stores in packs of ten colours)
- paper and pens
- the words of the message (below) written on a flashcard
- written instructions for heat-setting the T-shirt design (to take home)

Time required

60 minutes

Message

Following Jesus leads to everlasting life.

With your group

1. Read the Bible verse or play a game for the children to discover and read the verse. (See page 55).

   Jesus encouraged people to follow him. From this Bible verse, what did he promise to those who followed him?

2. Show the message too briefly for the group to take it in. Ask if anyone can repeat it. Keep flashing the message until they get it right and can say it together.

3. **We can encourage other people to follow Jesus by spreading the message that following Jesus leads to everlasting life. Jesus told his disciples to go to the whole world and tell people what he had taught them. When we tell others about Jesus, we're doing what he told his disciples, his followers, to do.**

4. Distribute the pens and paper for the children to design a 'logo' for the front of their T-shirt. Suggest that they keep it simple, such as a plain cross or a drawing of a Bible, so that it stands out. They could talk about their design with the person next to them, or with the group as a whole and discuss how it might be improved.

TIP

Decide on the best way to have a T-shirt available for everyone to decorate. Sometimes you can get a good deal by purchasing a large quantity. You could either take the money from club funds or send a note home asking for reimbursement. You may prefer to leave it up to each family to arrange their own. If so, send a note home with the children at least a week before you plan to carry out this activity, asking them to bring a plain white or light coloured T-shirt. Mention that they will be using T-shirt markers and may want to wear old clothes.

Follow me

5. Give out the T-shirt markers and allow time for everyone to transfer their design to their T-shirt. Warn them to keep the markers away from their clothes.

6. On the back of their T-shirt, the children could write their own message or slogan. Allow a few minutes to draw up a list of suggestions like 'I'm following Jesus' 'Follow the Leader' or 'Jesus leads. I follow'.

   Write them on a whiteboard or paper so that the children have the correct spelling.

7. When everyone has finished, remind them that their designs will need to be heat-set with an iron before washing the T-shirt. Hand out written instructions to take home.

8. Encourage children and leaders to express honestly their expectations and fears about following Jesus and conclude with the prayer.

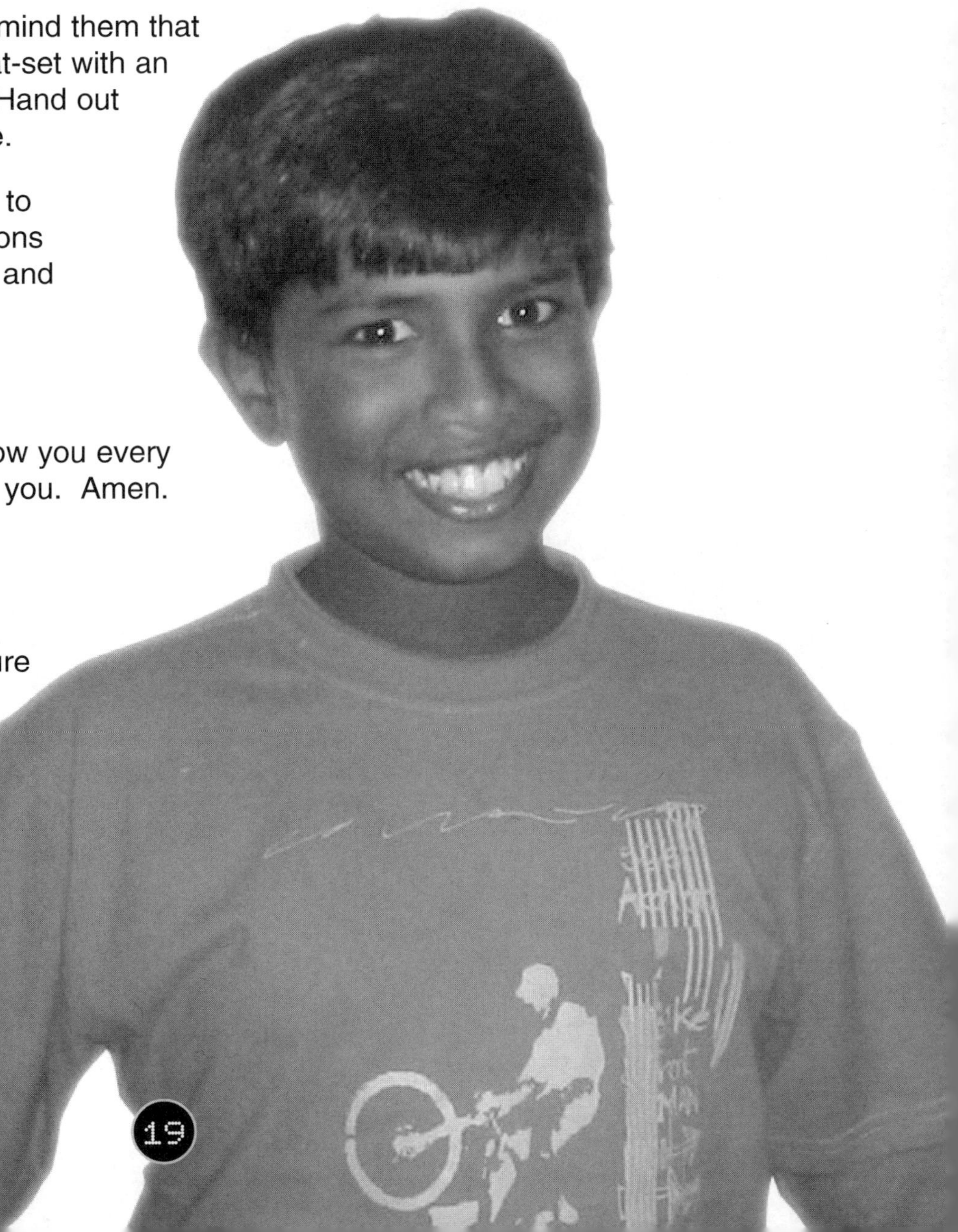

Prayer

Lord, please give us courage to follow you every day. Help us to lead other people to you. Amen.

Make it better

Talk together about a common feature that everyone could add to their shirt to identify them with the club. It could be

- the club name
- a common colour
- the same slogan
- an agreed club logo

Knocking

This handy door hanger encourages children to maintain contact with God.

Bible reading

Matthew 7:7,8 *Ask, and you will receive. Search, and you will find. Knock, and the door will be opened for you. Everyone who asks will receive. Everyone who searches will find. And the door will be opened for everyone who knocks.*

You will need

- one door hanger shape for each child
- scissors
- coloured marker pens
- clear contact
- glue sticks
- glitter glue, sequins, foil stars, etc. to decorate
- the words of the prayer written on paper

Cut rectangles measuring about 25 cm by 10 cm from heavy card with a hole at one end so it will fit over a door knob. Alternatively, plain wooden hangers can be purchased from many craft shops.

Time required

45 minutes

Message

God's door is always open to us.

With your group

1. Set up a regular rhythm with the group clapping or clicking. Read the Bible verse to the rhythm several times, inviting the children to join in as they are able.

2. **Imagine you are in a building you've never seen before. You come to a closed door. You hear someone say 'come in'. What's stopping you?** It's the closed door. You can only go in through an open door.

   People who have chosen to follow Jesus have opened the door to a new life. The door between them and God has been opened. When we belong to God the door between us and God is always open. Whenever we need God, he is there. When we want to talk to him about our worries, he welcomes us. He never closes the door on us. It is like having a best friend who is always home when we knock on their door. God wants us to be close to him. An important part of that is praying and reading the Bible.

3. Say the message aloud to the children. In groups of three or four challenge them to find a way to present the message in mime, charade or sign language to the bigger group. (Allow 5 minutes.)

4. Distribute the blank door hangers, along with the coloured marker pens, glue sticks, glitter glue, foil stars, sequins, etc.

on heaven's door

5. Copy the following onto the whiteboard:

    - Quiet please! Bible study in progress.
    - Wait your turn. My Friend is here.
    - Online with my Leader at present.
    - Please knock! It's my prayer time.

    Ask the group if they can think of any other slogans to write on the 'come in' side of their door hangers. When they have finished decorating them, cover the hangers with clear contact and trim neatly.

6. Conclude by inviting people to read the prayer silently or aloud together.

Prayer

Father God, we're glad that we can call on you at all times. Thank you that you always invite us and never turn us away. Amen.

8

Make this decorated egg as an Easter reminder of God's sacrifice.

Bible reading

John 3:16,17 *God loved the people of this world so much that he gave his only Son, so that everyone who has faith in him will have eternal life and never really die. God did not send his Son into the world to condemn its people. He sent him to save them!*

1 John 4:9,10 *God showed his love for us when he sent his only Son into the world to give us life. Real love isn't our love for God, but his love for us. God sent his Son to be the sacrifice by which our sins are forgiven.*

You will need

- One blown egg for each child
- PVA glue
- coloured marker pens
- acrylic paints (assorted colours)
- paintbrushes
- air-drying clay
- fine, narrow braid
- sequins, tiny stickers, glitter glue

Time required

45 minutes

Message

We can live a new life by believing in Jesus and living for him.

TIP

Send a note home with each child the week before this activity, asking them to bring a blown egg. If you have a small class, you might prefer to prepare them yourself. Have some spare eggs in case of accidents.

With your group

1. Read aloud the Bible verses and briefly encourage the children to share what Easter means to them.

2. **An egg doesn't look very alive, but if it is allowed to grow and develop naturally it will produce new life – a chicken or an eagle or a crocodile, depending on what sort of egg it is.**

   At Easter, Christians think a lot about Jesus and new life. Jesus died for us but God gave Jesus a new life by bringing him back to life after he was dead. Now we can share Jesus' new life.

   When we choose to follow Jesus Christ, God forgives our sins and gives us new life which lasts forever, even after we die. Jesus is the most important part of our new life. He is beside us, at home, school, and wherever we go. He helps us to make the right choices throughout our new life.

3. Write the message on the whiteboard and leave it on display.

To make blown eggs, use a needle to make a hole through each end of the shell. Widen it as necessary until the contents start to ooze out. Blow hard into one end until the egg empties. Soak the blown eggs in warm, soapy water, then leave to dry overnight. Handle them carefully as they are extremely

New Life

4. Put all the materials on a table and let the children decorate their egg with the coloured markers, warning them to handle them very carefully. Give them some ideas, such as the words 'new life', or 'Jesus lives'. They can add other decorations as they choose.

The clay baskets will take 24 hours to dry at room temperature. They can be painted before they dry.

5. When they have finished, have them coat their eggs with PVA glue (this will give the eggs a shiny appearance once dry). Set the eggs aside on a sheet of white paper.

6. Distribute the air-drying clay (a piece the size of a golf ball is sufficient) for the children to make a small basket for their egg. They can then paint it and put their decorated egg inside.

7. Encourage the children to hold their eggs and silently tell God what his death and new life means to them, then conclude with the prayer.

Prayer

Almighty God, you sacrificed your Son so our sins could be forgiven. We praise your name and worship you always.
Amen.

Make it easier

Instead of using real eggs, the children could make small ones from air-drying clay.

9

With this scroll, children can create a work of art and think about making a commitment to God.

Bible reading

John 15:4-5 *Stay joined to me, and I will stay joined to you. Just as a branch cannot produce fruit unless it stays joined to the vine, you cannot produce fruit unless you stay joined to me. I am the vine, and you are the branches. If you stay joined to me, and I stay joined to you, then you will produce lots of fruit. But you cannot do anything without me.*

You will need

- mock parchment paper
- paintbrushes (fine tipped)
- gold acrylic paint
- coloured marker pens
- 20 cm of red ribbon for each child

To make mock parchment paper for the scrolls, put white paper in the oven for 30 minutes at 180 °C to give it a golden brown tint.

Time required

30 minutes

Message

God loves us to commit ourselves to him.

With your group

1. Explain that the Bible passage uses the words 'fruit' and 'branches' and 'vine' but it's not talking about plants. Challenge them to work out what it's really about as they listen. Read the Bible passage to the children.

   What do you think God is trying to tell us in these verses? Accept answers.

   Staying joined to God is about being committed to God and living to please him. It's about letting him live his life through us. To do that, we need to be saying yes to what he wants us to do. We need to invite him to be involved in every part of our life. Reading the Bible and talking to God is one way we stay joined to him.

2. Display the message.

3. **In Washington DC, America there is a document called the Declaration of Independence which was written in 1776 to declare that certain things would be done from then on and people could depend on it. We can make a declaration too. God is pleased when we commit ourselves to live for him. If you've done that or are ready to, you could write a declaration of faith, listing things that you will do because you are committed to God. Some people are still thinking about God and what to do about living for Jesus. If that's you, you could make a declaration that you'll try hard to find out all you can so you will make the right decision.**

Sign me up

4. Distribute the materials for making the scrolls. Encourage the children to write their own declaration, but have some options on the whiteboard for them to use as a model. For example

   I _________________(name) declare that I will find out what the Bible says about God and life and me.

   I ____________(name) promise and declare that I will try to faithfully follow the teaching of the Bible and hereby commit myself to serving God.

   I _____________(name) declare that I want to get to know God better and stay joined to him. I'll do that by trying to read the Bible and pray every day.

5. Using the coloured marker pens, the children should write their scrolls in decorative lettering. When they have finished, they can use the gold paint and fine-tipped brushes to outline and enhance capital letters and paint a border around the edges of the scroll.

6. Invite the children to look at their scroll and silently say something to God about what they have written. Conclude by choosing a volunteer to read the prayer.

TIP

When the paint is completely dry on the scrolls, roll them up, tie a piece of red ribbon around each one, and they are ready for the children to take home.

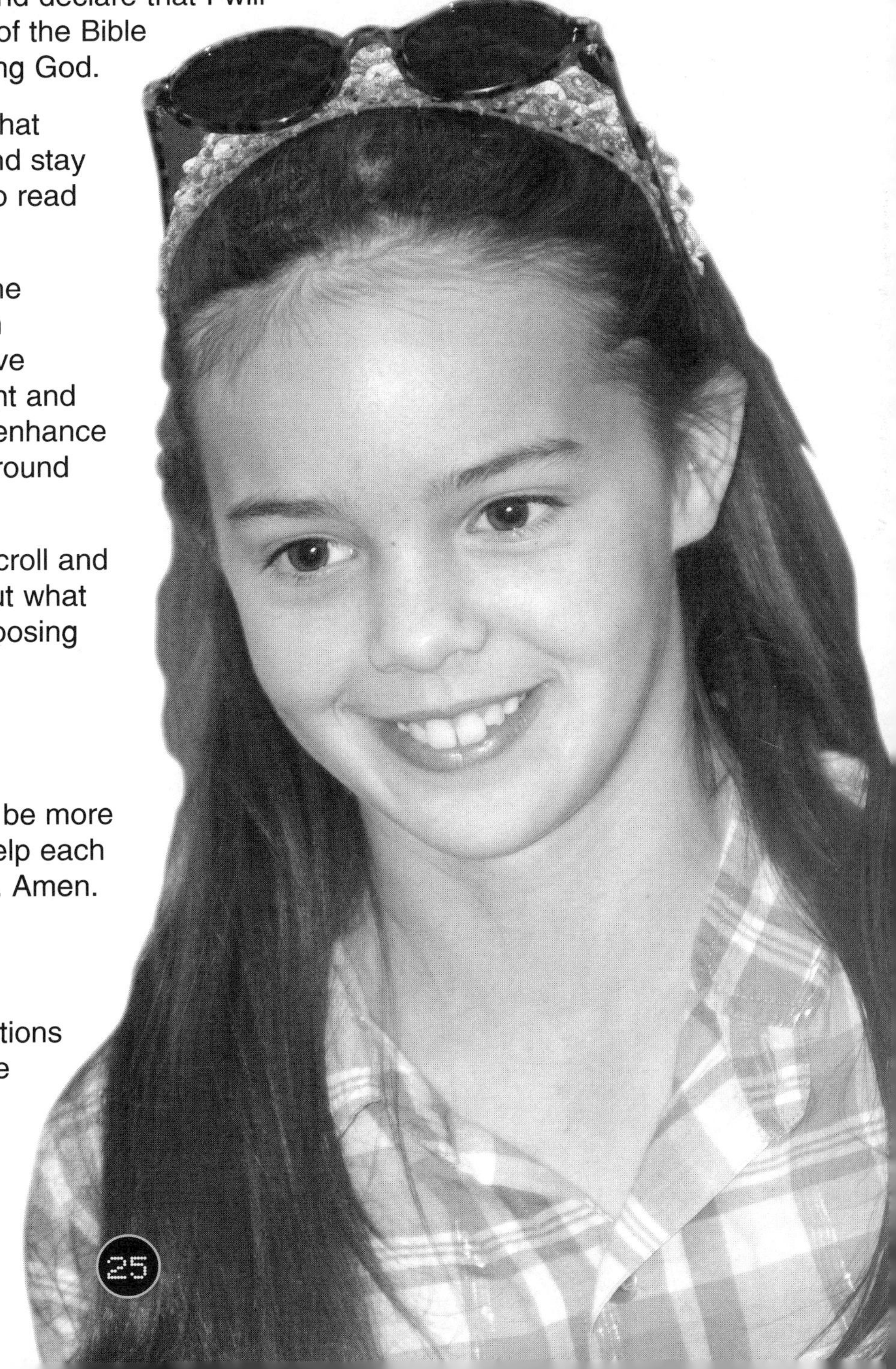

Prayer

Dear God, help us all to take a step to be more committed to you. Please help us to help each other to keep our commitments to you. Amen.

Make it easier

You could print out a choice of declarations in fancy fonts with open lettering so the children only have to decorate rather than write. But make sure there is something they can truthfully commit to. God loves us to be honest.

13

A little

These quick and easy fridge magnets provide an important reminder to pray every day.

Bible readings

Philippians 4:6,7 *Don't worry about anything, but pray about everything. With thankful hearts offer up your prayers and requests to God. Then, because you belong to Christ Jesus, God will bless you with peace that no one can completely understand. And this peace will control the way you think and feel.*

Psalm 86:5-7 *You willingly forgive, and your love is always there for those who pray to you. Please listen, Lord! Answer my prayer for help. When I am in trouble, I pray, knowing you will listen.*

Materials

- magnet sheets cut into 2 cm squares
- craft glue
- coloured card
- clear contact
- coloured marker pens
- scissors
- small stickers

Magnet sheets are available from craft stores.

Time required

20 to 30 minutes

Message

God listens when we pray sincerely to him.

With your group

1. Choose volunteers to read the Bible verses.
2. **When we pray, we talk directly to God.**

   By praying and sharing our life with God in prayer, our relationship with God will grow stronger.

   Deliberately ignoring or going against God harms that relationship.
3. Say the message aloud. Ask the group what they think it means to pray sincerely.
4. Explain that you'll be making your own fridge magnet to remind you to pray. Ask the children to think of some suitable slogans which would remind them to pray. Write their suggestions on the whiteboard.

reminder

5. Distribute the coloured card, marker pens and stickers. Encourage the children to write a slogan on the card, decorate it and cut it into the shape they want. They can then cover the front with clear contact and glue the magnet to the back.

   Some children may need help to get it smooth.

TIP

Cut the contact just a little larger than the card. Place the decorated card face up on a firm surface, and smooth the contact over the top using both hands. Trim.

6. As the children are creating their fridge magnets, talk about prayer. Share your experiences honestly and encourage them to do the same. Discussion could include things like:

   Things that help us to pray
   - Finding our own time and place
   - Taking our worries to God
   - Including God in our exciting moments
   - Using a prayer book

   Things that can stop us praying
   - What to do when we feel God isn't listening
   - Confessing sins and being forgiven
   - How to remember to pray

   Different types of prayer
   - Thank you
   - Sorry
   - Please
   - Praying 'in our head'
   - Shouting

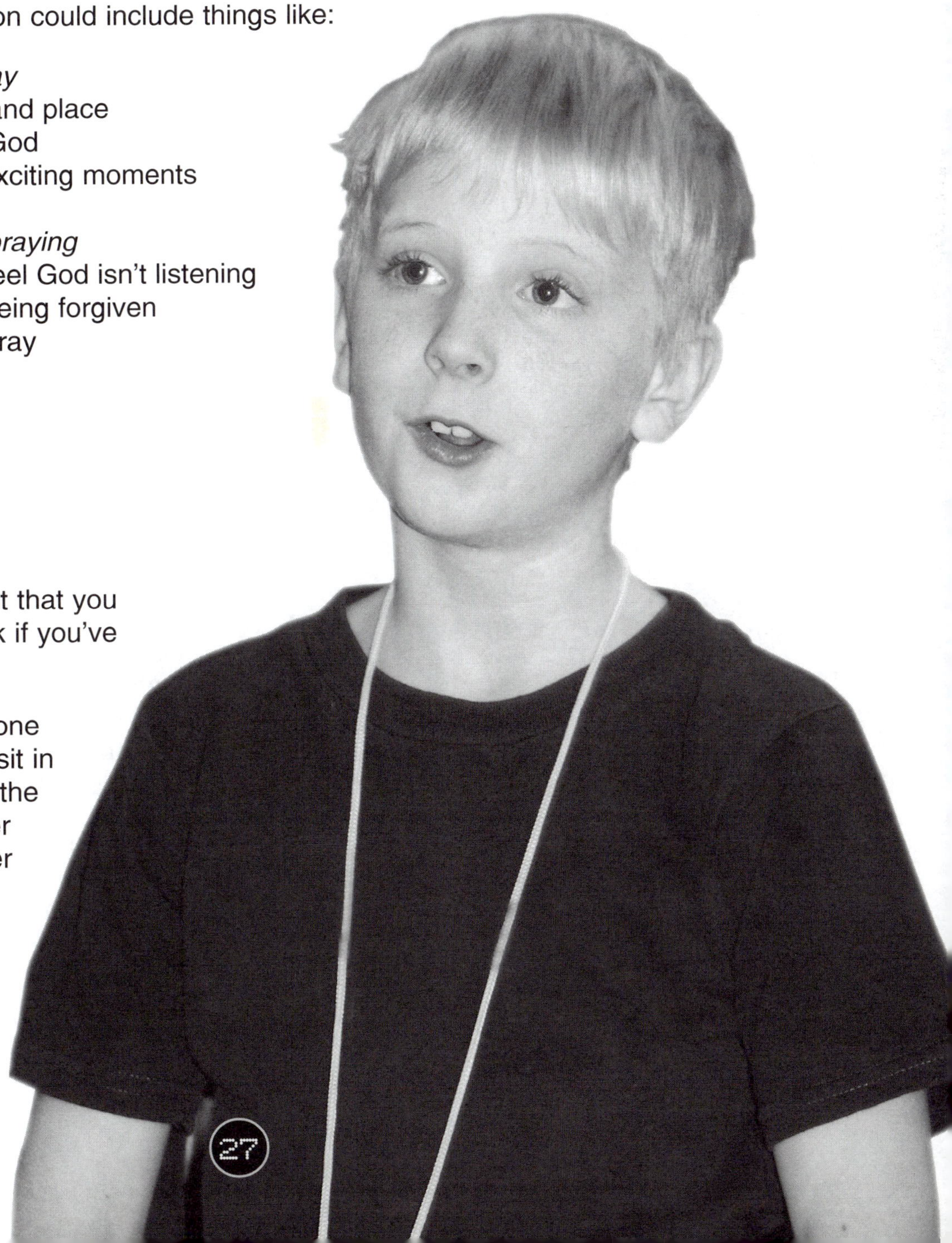

6. If it's appropriate, suggest that you ask each other next week if you've been praying more.

7. Since this is about everyone praying more, you could sit in a circle (or stand around the table) and pray the prayer quickly one after the other without a break.

Prayer

Thank you for listening to our prayers. Please help us all to pray more. Amen.

11

Make this window decoration to remind the children that God sends his angels to watch over and protect us. It's a good choice for a Christmas craft or for any time of year.

Bible reading

Psalm 91:11 *God will command his angels to protect you wherever you go.*

Psalm 34:7 *If you honour the Lord, his angel will protect you.*

You will need

- one copy of the angel template from page 30 for each child
- one A4 plastic sheet protector (plastic sleeve) for each child
- glass paint (assorted colours, including white, flesh colour, black and gold)
- adhesive tape

Time required

30 minutes

Message

God's angels watch over us.

With your group

1. Ask the children to guess the day's theme as they listen to the two Bible verses. Invite two volunteers to read Psalm 91:11 and Psalm 34:7.

2. **There are examples throughout the Bible of angels appearing, carrying out God's commands.** See how many the group can recall, for example, it was an angel that gave Mary the news that she was to give birth to Jesus (Luke 1:26-28) and an angel that told that Jesus was alive again (Matthew 28:1-4) .

   Angels are heavenly beings who serve God. They are God's messengers.

   Humans can't call or control them. They obey only God.

   Angels protect God's people from harm.

3. Write the message on the whiteboard and invite the children to say it aloud.

4. Distribute the sheet protectors with copies of the angel template inside. Show how to use the black glass paint, following the template to outline the angel's body, head, hair, wings, robes, and hands. Then, using the other colours, fill in the spaces until the angel is completely coloured in with paint.

5. When complete, carefully stick the sheet protectors to a window with tape. Gather the group around the window and pray together.

Guardian angel

Prayer

Almighty God, we are glad you watch over and protect us. We thank you for sending your angels to keep us safe.
Amen.

TIP

The children will need to take their angels home on the plastic sheet protectors as they take six hours to dry fully. They can then be peeled off and stuck to any glass surface.

Children who finish quickly could see what they can discover about angels visiting people from these verses:

- Matthew 28:1-4
- Acts 5:17-21
- Acts 27:23
- Exodus 3:1-2
- 1 Kings 19:5-8

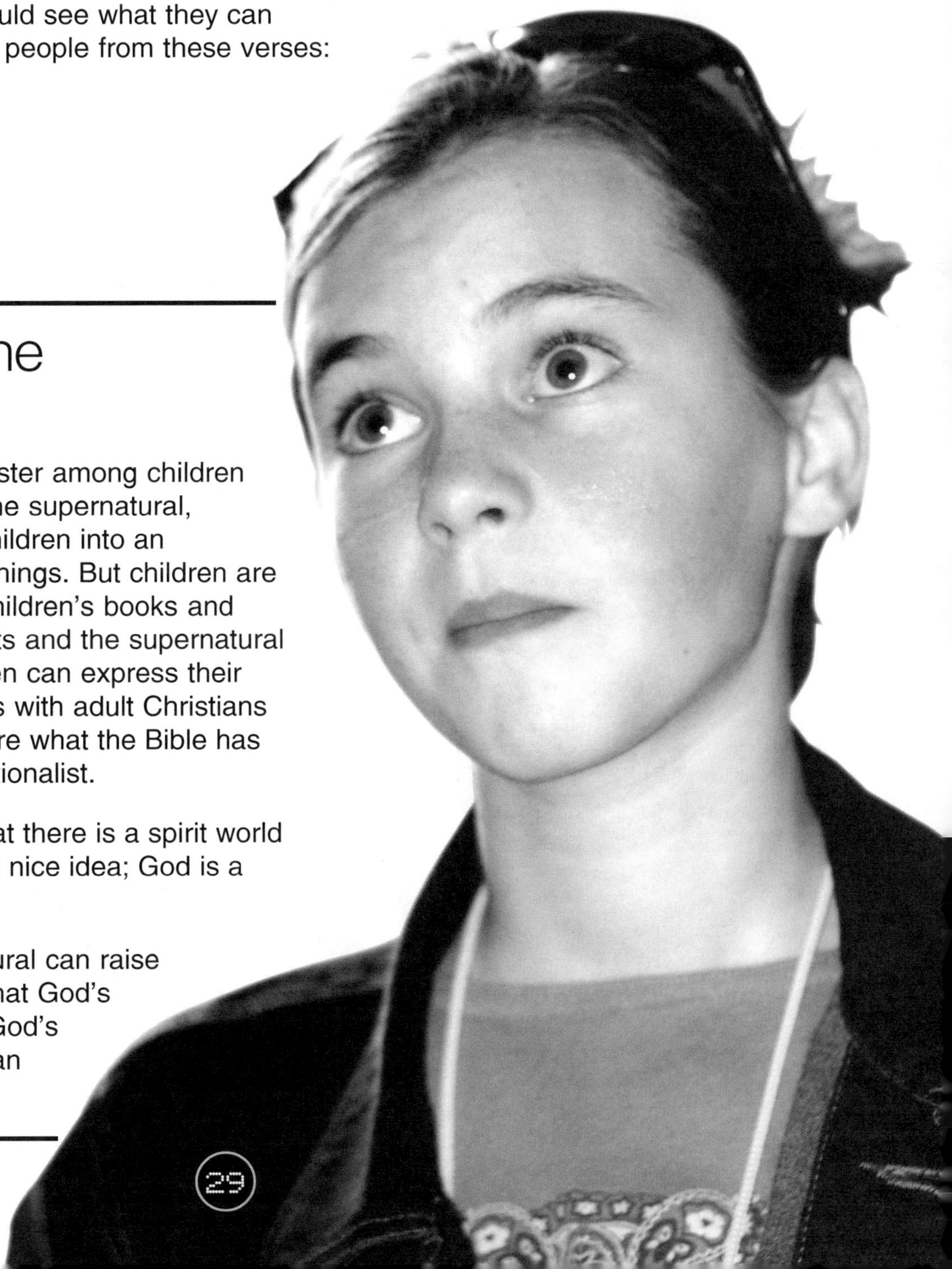

Children and the supernatural

Sometimes those who minister among children shy away from talk about the supernatural, worried that it could lead children into an unhealthy interest in such things. But children are already interested. Many children's books and movies involve magic, spirits and the supernatural so it's important that children can express their thoughts about these things with adult Christians who will lead them to explore what the Bible has to say without being sensationalist.

The Bible makes it clear that there is a spirit world that's real. God is not just a nice idea; God is a supernatural being.

Talking about the supernatural can raise fears in children so affirm that God's Holy Spirit who lives in all God's people is more powerful than any spirit and protects us.

Faith Shapers

THE 10 COMMANDMENTS

DO NOT WORSHIP ANY OTHER GOD EXCEPT THE ONE TRUE GOD.

DO NOT MAKE OR WORSHIP IDOLS.

DO NOT MISUSE GOD'S NAME.

KEEP GOD'S DAY SPECIAL.
DON'T DO ANY WORK ON IT.

RESPECT YOUR PARENTS.

DO NOT MURDER.

BE FAITHFUL IN MARRIAGE.

DO NOT STEAL.

DO NOT TELL LIES ABOUT OTHERS.

DO NOT WANT ANYTHING THAT BELONGS TO SOMEONE ELSE.

12

Making this jigsaw will encourage the children to remember God's rules for living.

Bible reading

Exodus 20:1-17 The Ten Commandments

God said to the people of Israel:
I am the Lord your God, the one who brought you out of Egypt where you were slaves. Do not worship any god except me.
… Don't bow down and worship idols.
I am the Lord your God, and I demand all your love.
Do not misuse my name. I am the Lord your God, and I will punish anyone who misuses my name.
Remember that the Sabbath Day belongs to me.
You have six days when you can do your work, but the seventh day of each week belongs to me, your God.
No one is to work on that day.
Respect your father and your mother, and you will live a long time in the land I am giving you.
Do not murder.
Be faithful in marriage.
Do not steal.
Do not tell lies about others.
Do not want anything that belongs to someone else.
Don't want anyone's house, wife or husband, slaves, oxen, donkeys or anything else.

You will need

- a copy of page 31 to display
- one heavyweight coloured card sheet about 42 cm by 30 cm for each child
- heavy duty scissors
- coloured marker pens
- small freezer or sandwich bags for the children to take their puzzle pieces home.

TIP

To display the Ten Commandments, enlarge page 31 on a photocopier or copy it onto acetate and use an overhead projector.

Time required

30 minutes

Message

We can please God by obeying his rules.

With your group

1. Choose a volunteer to read aloud the Bible passage. Display the Ten Commandments from page 31.

2. **These Ten Commandments are laws that God gave his people thousands of years ago. But they are more than just a set of rules. They help us know what to do to live well, so we don't spoil our lives.**

   Which ones help us get on better with other people?

   Which ones help us get on better with God?

   Keeping these rules shows that we want to be God's people and please him.

3. Write the message on the whiteboard and invite the group to say it aloud.

4. Distribute the card, coloured markers and scissors for the children to make the basis of their jigsaw. They can leave their card as a rectangle or cut it into the shape of a stone tablet. Encourage them to copy some of the Commandments (or all ten if they prefer) onto the card and add borders or decorate it.

Bits and pieces

5. As each person finishes, they can cut their card into forty, even-sized pieces to produce a jigsaw. Have them mix the pieces up and give them to another group member to put the jigsaw together. When everyone has finished, give each child a bag to put the pieces in to take home.
6. Conclude by reading the prayer.

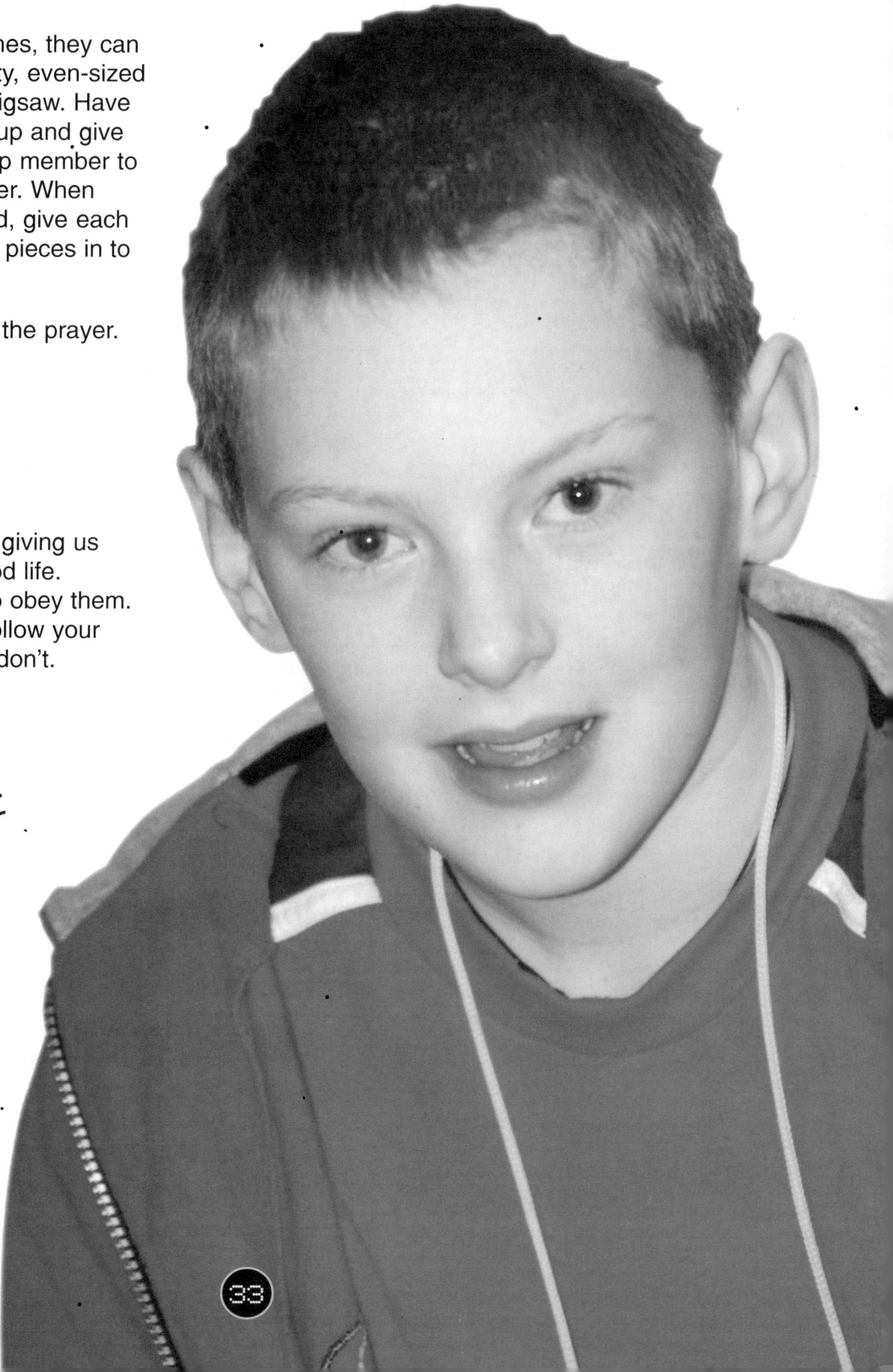

Prayer

Lord God, Thank you for giving us your rules for living a good life. Please help us to want to obey them. Give us the courage to follow your rules, even when others don't. Amen.

Make it easier

A guillotine makes it easier to cut through heavy cardboard. It's not safe for most children to use so cut the children's puzzles for them and keep the guillotine out of reach and out of sight when you are not using it.

13

Children can talk informally about God's creation of the world as they make this harvest wreath.

Bible reading

This is the key verse but choose as much or as little from Psalm 104:1-30 as your group will appreciate.

Psalm 104:24 *Our Lord, by your wisdom you made so many things; the whole earth is covered with your living creatures.*

You will need

- a cardboard wreath base for each child
- hot glue gun
- dried flowers, leaves, seed pods, gum nuts, pine cones
- scissors
- spray varnish – gloss (available from craft and hardware stores)
- paintbrushes

Time required

40 minutes

Message

In the beginning God created the heavens and the earth.

With your group

1. **God made a truly marvellous earth for us to live on.**

   There are around 750,000 different kinds of insects, 25,000 different kinds of fish and 9,000 different kinds of birds. And that's just the ones that have been discovered so far!

   Imagine supplying everything those creatures need every day. The earth has 400,000 different kinds of plants, so all living things have the type of food and shelter they need.

   Psalm 104 and the beginning of the Bible book of Genesis describe the creation of our world. God planned for the earth to be a paradise for his people, filled with natural wonders and amazing creatures. Ask the children to think of some examples.

Prepare the wreath bases from thick cardboard. Packing boxes are ideal. Use a dinner plate to make the outer circle the correct size, then cut an inner circle using a smaller plate. Cut out and discard the inner circle so that you have a cardboard hoop.

2. Read the Bible verse(s) to the group.

3. One of the fascinating things about the world is the way God keeps it going. The things God made in the beginning are not on earth now, but living things have built-in ways of producing more of themselves so they continue on and on.

   Plants produce so much fruit and seed that people can harvest them for food and there's still plenty left. That's one way God provides food for people and animals.

4. Distribute the seed pods, pine cones and other natural materials. Pull apart some of

God's harvest

the pinecones or seed pods and get excited together about how many seeds a whole tree can produce every year. Marvel at the way a huge tree started out as a tiny seed.

Say the message aloud and invite the children to repeat it with you.

5. Show how to make a harvest wreath in celebration of God's creation. Demonstrate how to use the glue gun safely and warn everyone to be careful of the liquid glue as it is very hot.

   When the wreaths are complete, varnish them in a well ventilated room, or preferably outside.

6. Ask everyone to think of something God has made that they specially like. Stand in a circle. Ask for a volunteer to start off the prayer, then go around the circle with each person adding what they like.

Prayer

Creator God, thank you for giving us our beautiful world with all its wonders to enjoy, especially … Amen.

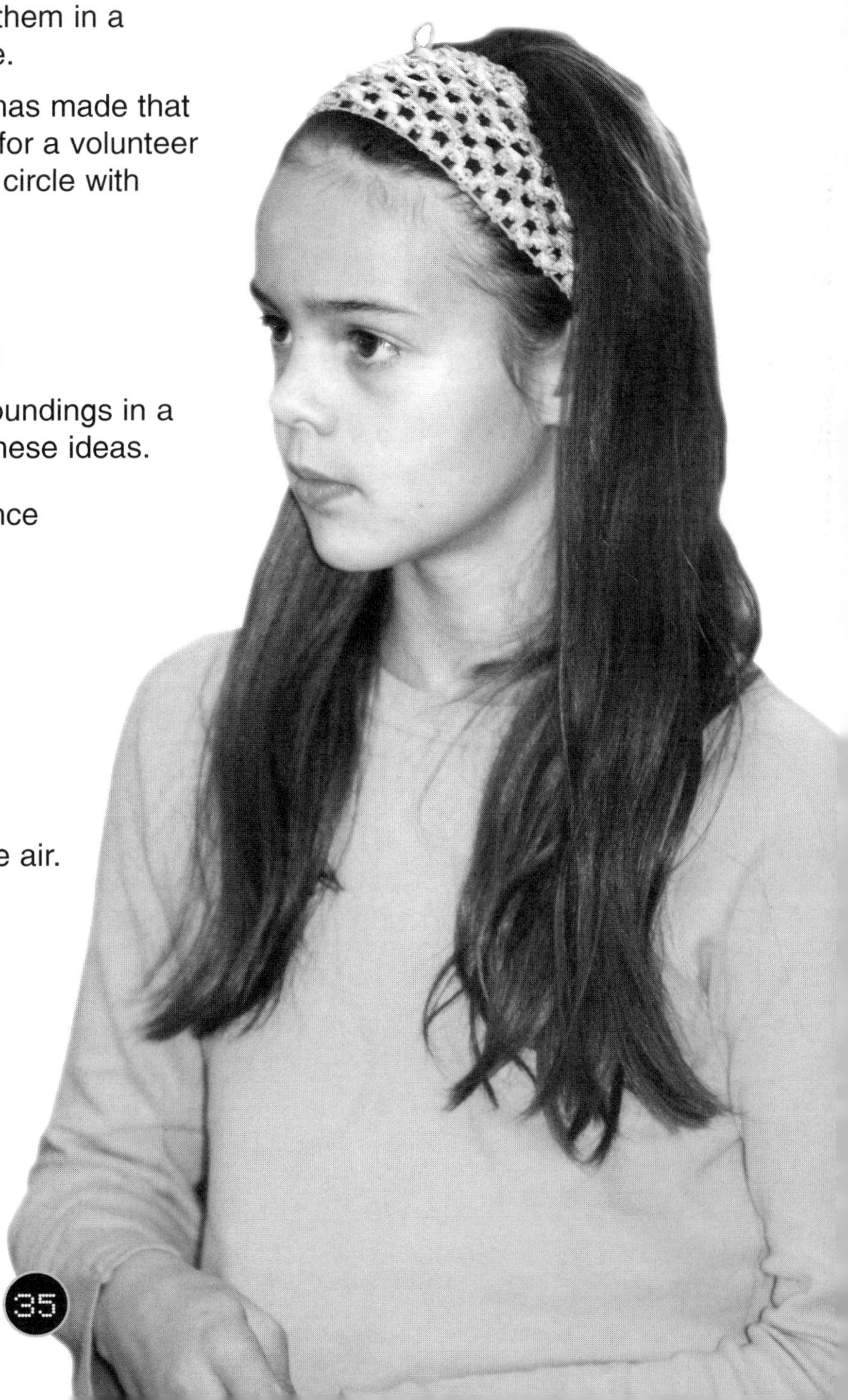

Make it better (outdoors)

Take your group outside to explore their surroundings in a way that is safe and practical. Choose from these ideas.

Lie on the grass and watch the clouds in silence for one minute or more.

Listen with your eyes shut.

Dig to see what's underground.

Close your eyes and feel grass, tree trunks and other interesting textures.

Close your eyes and smell plants, soil and the air.

Make it better (indoors)

As a way of enjoying the variety of God's creation, give each group of two or three children a piece of paper and pen and challenge them to write down the name of a plant or animal beginning with every letter of the alphabet.

14

This greeting card doubles as an invitation to hear about Jesus and creates an opportunity for the children to think about sharing their faith.

Bible reading

Philippians 2:6-11 *Christ was truly God. But he did not try to remain equal with God. He gave up everything and became a slave, when he became like one of us. Christ was humble. He obeyed God and even died on a cross. Then God gave Christ the highest place and honoured his name above all others. So at the name of Jesus everyone will bow down, those in heaven, on earth, and under the earth. And to the glory of God the Father everyone will openly agree, 'Jesus Christ is Lord!'*

You will need

- pre cut cards
- glue sticks
- scraps of felt or funky foam
- coloured marker pens
- scissors

Use heavyweight card especially designed for card making. It is sold in packs and available in plain and metallic colours.

TIP

Have a correction pen on hand to cover any mistakes when the cards are being written.

Time required

30 minutes

Message

By sharing our faith, we can help to bring others closer to God.

With your group

1. Read the Bible passage aloud asking the group beforehand to listen for what it tells about Jesus. Share what you all discovered.

2. **Many people have not heard these things about Jesus. They haven't had the chance to know how good it is to live a life of faith with Jesus as their friend.**

3. Talk with the group about how their friends or others they know could be given the chance to find out about Jesus. Plan a special group meeting, a chance for them to start to share with others what it is like to have faith.

   Decide when and where it should be and what the program should contain. Write details on the whiteboard. Challenge the group to think of ways they could share their faith through such an event.

4. Give everyone a card and let them create a picture on the front to appeal to their friend, using scraps of felt or funky foam. Offer some suggestions for the design, such as a stylised flower, a cheerful sun with a smiling face or an abstract design. Allow about 20 minutes for this.

   Copy the time and place details from the whiteboard.

   Ask the children to think about the person they would like to give their card to and write a personal message inside the card, inviting that person to the special group meeting. Emphasise that God welcomes everyone so we need to as well. They might decide to invite someone who rarely gets invitations.

   Help with spelling and grammar as needed.

5. Choose a volunteer to read the prayer, or encourage those who wish, to pray for their friends

Spread the word

Prayer

Lord, help us to bring our friends to learn about you, so that they can share in your love.
Amen.

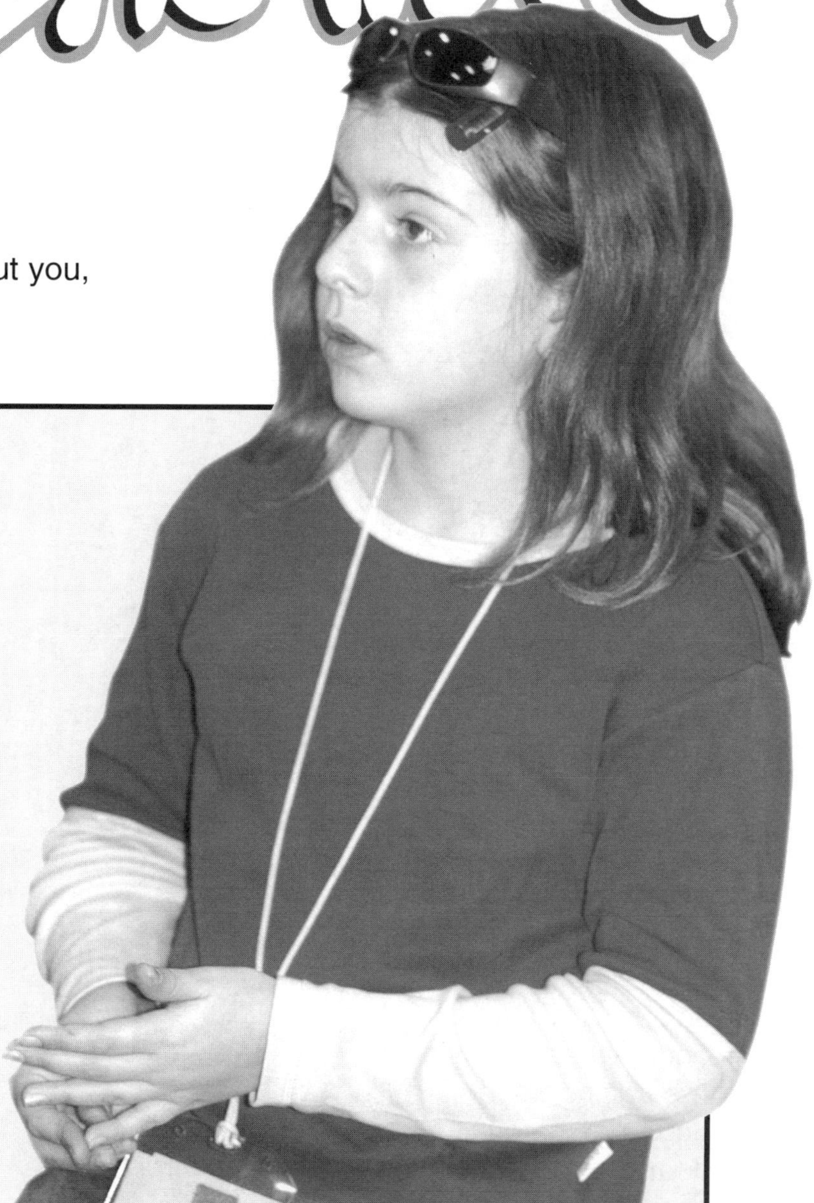

Think ahead

Introducing others to Jesus is a process, and often a lengthy one.

It is most effective when someone has a chance to build a relationship of trust and can share their life with another, giving them the chance to observe what it means to live as a Christian and ask questions in the course of everyday life.

Sometimes we talk about what God is doing in our life with those who share our beliefs but wouldn't dream of talking in the same way with those who don't. Or we share with fellow leaders how difficult it is to find time to read our Bible or live as we know we should, but with our groups we cover up the difficulties.

Working on a craft project with the children can allow you to share your faith. When for example, you make a fridge magnet to remind you to pray, chat about where you'll put it and why. Then the children realise that you too are on a spiritual journey and haven't yet 'arrived'.

Practice being open about your faith, warts and all. Model a natural way of sharing with others, whoever the others are. Develop within your group a culture of speaking about the spiritual side of life, just as you do about events and fashions.

Don't try to be deep and meaningful and cover everything in one go. Be prepared to leave questions hanging and move onto other topics as the conversation progresses.

Be more prepared to ask 'What do you think?' and 'Has anything like that ever happened to you?' than to tell your own story.

Your group may be the only place these young people get the chance to freely talk about faith issues.

15

Celebrate the birth of our Saviour with these Christmas tree decorations made from display dough.

Bible reading

Luke 2:11 *This very day in King David's hometown a Saviour was born for you. He is Christ the Lord.*

If your group is not familiar with the narrative of Jesus birth, you could read more from Luke 2.

You will need

- display dough the size of a tennis ball for each child (recipe on page 4)
- plastic knives
- acrylic paints (assorted colours)
- paintbrushes
- wooden skewers
- rolling pins
- large baking trays
- baking parchment
- folk art varnish (gloss) or clear wood varnish
- Christmas cookie cutters (optional)
- Paper and pens
- CD of Christmas carols and CD player (optional)

Time required

45 minutes

Message

Listen up. Lend an ear
Christmas time is very near.
Celebrate the Saviour's birth
Jesus Christ was born on earth.

With your group

1. Read the Bible verse aloud. Play the Christmas music and distribute the paper and pens. Display the message and read it aloud. Ask the children to write their own message, as a verse or in rap style, working in pairs or threes. Allow about ten minutes for this. Invite them to read their messages aloud to the group.

2. **To a lot of people Christmas is just about presents and food and holidays.**

   For others there's much more to it.

   Christmas is about Jesus being born in Bethlehem, the most important event in history, the one our calendar starts with.

   But there's even more to it.

   Jesus wasn't just a baby who grew to be a very wise man. He came from heaven to live and die for us so we could be freed from our sins and live as God's friends forever.

   Think about shapes and symbols you could make as a reminder of this deeper meaning of Christmas.

> **TIP**
>
> *If the dough sticks to the rolling pin, sprinkle a little flour on it.*

Christmas creations

3. Distribute the display dough (a tennis ball sized piece is adequate to make three decorations each), wooden skewers, rolling pins and plastic knives. Instruct the children to roll out their dough to about 0.75 cm thickness and carefully cut out shapes that will remind those who see them of the coming of Jesus to be our Saviour.

   They could make angels, stars, Jesus in the manger, Mary and Joseph.

   Alternatively, they could use the cookie cutters.

4. The children will need to make a hole about 0.5 cm wide in the top of each item using the skewers, then paint their decorations using the acrylic paints. The painted decorations should be placed carefully on lined baking trays.

   The decorations will need to be baked for nine hours at 120 °C/gas mark 0.5.

   When dry, they will need a coat of varnish.

5. As the children complete their decorations and wait for others to finish, they might like to add a Christmas prayer and Christmas symbols to a large sheet of paper to make a prayer poster.

6. Conclude with the prayer.

Prayer

Gracious God, we thank you
for the wonderful gift of
Jesus, our Saviour.
Amen.

16

The life of Jesus can be celebrated by these wall hangings made from fabric.

Bible reading

John 6:38-40 *(Jesus said) 'I didn't come from heaven to do what I want! I came to do what the Father wants me to do. He sent me, and he wants to make certain that none of the ones he has given me will be lost. Instead, he wants me to raise them to life on the last day. My Father wants everyone who sees the Son to have faith in him and to have eternal life. Then I will raise them to life on the last day.'*

You will need

- rectangles of calico or similar cotton fabric (50 cm by 30 cm)
- PVA glue
- fabric scraps of varied colours
- funky foam
- scissors
- pens
- coloured marker pens

Time required

45 to 60 minutes

Message

Jesus lived for God on earth and is alive forever.

TIP

Put a request in your church newsletter for fabric scraps. Ask for a volunteer to hem them or cut them to size with pinking scissors to prevent fraying.

TIP

To minimise mess, put all the tables/desks together, with chairs around the outside. Put the fabric, scissors, glue and other materials in the middle.

With your group

1. Read the Bible verses aloud and explain that the aim of the session is to make a series of wall hangings to show the life of Jesus on earth. Different people will concentrate on doing different parts of Jesus' life.

2. Write the message on the whiteboard. With the group, quickly recall the significant events in Jesus' life.

   Make a list on the whiteboard.

   - The birth of Jesus
   - Jesus being baptised by John the Baptist
   - Healing the sick
   - Feeding the five thousand
   - Calming the storm
   - Jesus teaching
   - The last supper
   - Jesus on the cross
   - Jesus alive again
   - Jesus going up to heaven

Jesus lives

3. Ask the children to choose one of the events (Ensure that they choose different ones.) and create a picture using the fabric scraps and funky foam, cut into shapes and glued onto the background fabric. They can draw in faces and detail with coloured markers. Some children may need help with cutting the fabric.

   Display the separate hangings in order as they are finished, and ask the maker to tell a friend or the whole group about their hanging.

4. Invite the children to reflect for a few moments on all that Jesus was and did while he was on earth. Affirm that Jesus is alive forever and his Spirit is active on earth today through those who love him.

5. Conclude with the prayer. Encourage everyone to tell God how they feel about Jesus, either aloud or 'in their head'.

Prayer

Dear Jesus, our Saviour, We thank you for giving your life for us. We are glad you live forever in heaven and your Spirit is with us.
Amen.

Make it better!

The finished hangings will look much better if the 'people shapes' on them are large. Pre-cut tall triangles (about 18 cm high on a 12 cm base) in various colours and circles (about 6 cm in diameter) in natural colours for the children to use as the bodies and heads of their people.

17

Creating this mosaic picture will encourage children to think about who God is.

Bible reading

Acts 17:24-28a *This God made the world and everything in it. He is Lord of heaven and earth, and he doesn't live in temples built by human hands. He doesn't need help from anyone. He gives life, breath, and everything else to all people. From one person God made all nations who live on earth, and he decided when and where every nation would be.*

God has done all this, so that we will look for him and reach out and find him. He isn't far from any of us, and he gives us the power to live, to move, and to be who we are. 'We are his children,' just as some of your poets have said.

You will need

- One sheet of A4 card (30 cm by 21 cm) for each child
- gummed paper cut into squares measuring 2 cm by 2 cm (assorted colours)
- scissors
- coloured marker pens
- sponges (for moistening the gummed paper)

Time required

20 minutes

Message

God is always with us.

With your group

1. Read the Bible verses.
2. **How do you imagine God? Some people think of God with a human body, while others think of God as a presence around them. The Bible tells us that God is a spirit, which means he is invisible, but that he is close to each one of us. God is in heaven, but he is also active on earth. What did the Bible passage say about God?**
3. Give each child a piece of card, some gummed paper squares, coloured markers and scissors. Explain that they can make a mosaic picture of how they imagine God.

   Say the message aloud and invite the children to say it back to you.
4. Show the children how to draw their picture first on the card, then fill in the drawing with coloured squares. Any small details can be added afterwards with coloured markers. Talk with the children individually as they work on their picture and allow time at the end for those who want to tell about it.
5. When everyone has finished, display the pictures and choose a volunteer to read the prayer.

Young children usually have no trouble drawing God but as they get older and start to think abstractly, it becomes more difficult to put their thoughts on paper. Encourage older ones to use symbols, colours and words to represent feelings and abstract ideas.

Picture perfect

QUICK CRAFT – *20 minutes or less*

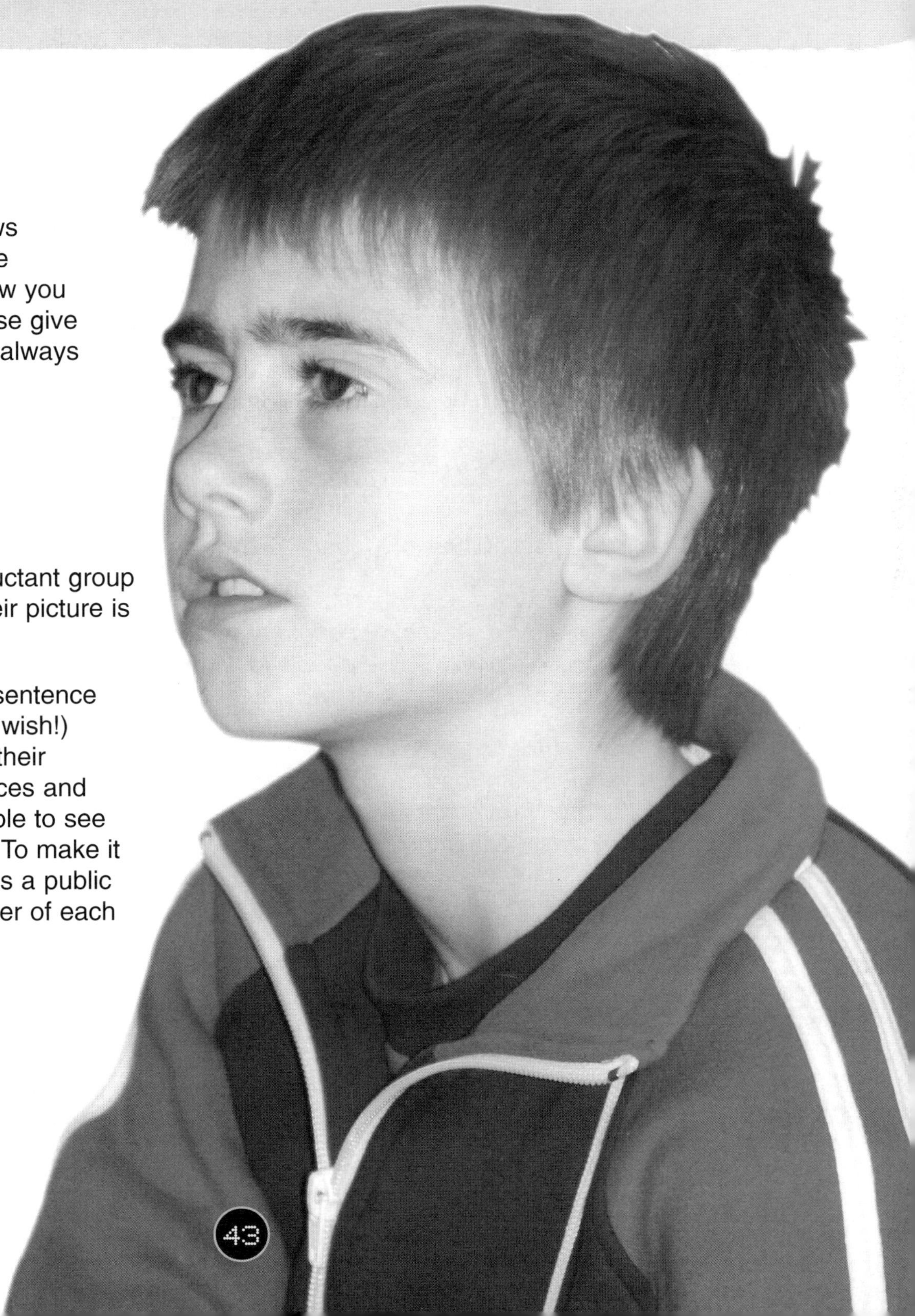

Prayer

Dear God, none of us knows exactly what you're like. We cannot see you but we know you are watching over us. Please give us confidence that you will always be with us. Amen.

Make it better!

Here's a way of getting reluctant group members to share what their picture is about.

Challenge them to write a sentence (in disguised writing if they wish!) which tells the meaning of their picture. Display the sentences and the pictures and invite people to see if they can match them up. To make it less threatening, pretend it's a public exhibition in which the maker of each picture is unknown.

18

This special gift uses a non-messy technique for making a papiér-maché...

flower pot

Bible reading

Luke 8:4-15 *When a large crowd from several towns had gathered around Jesus, he told them this story:*

A farmer went out to scatter seed in a field. While the farmer was doing it, some of the seeds fell along the road and were stepped on or eaten by birds. Other seeds fell on rocky ground and started growing. But the plants did not have enough water and soon dried up. Some other seeds fell where thornbushes grew up and choked the plants. The rest of the seeds fell on good ground where they grew and produced a hundred times as many seeds.

When Jesus had finished speaking, he said, 'If you have ears, pay attention!'

Jesus' disciples asked him what the story meant. So he answered:

I have explained the secrets about God's kingdom to you, but for others I can only use stories. These people look, but they don't see, and they hear, but they don't understand.

This is what the story means: The seed is God's message, and the seeds that fell along the road are the people who hear the message. But the devil comes and snatches the message out of their hearts, so that they will not believe and be saved. The seeds that fell on rocky ground are the people who gladly hear the message and accept it. But they don't have deep roots, and they believe only for a little while. As soon as life gets hard, they give up.

The seeds that fell among the thornbushes are also people who hear the message. But they are so eager for riches and pleasures that they never produce anything. Those seeds that fell on good ground are the people who listen to the message and keep it in good and honest hearts. They last and produce a harvest.

You will need

- one plastic cup for each child
- white scrap paper
- paintbrushes
- PVA glue
- acrylic paints (assorted colours)
- 6-8 flower seeds for each child
- potting mix

Time required

60 minutes

Message

By following God's teaching, our faith continues to grow.

Before you start covering it, poke a few holes in the bottom of the cup with a skewer.

Make if different

Instead of paint, coloured paper or patterned wrapping paper can be used. Give a final coat of PVA glue to seal.

Seeds of life

With your group

1. Ask a competent reader to read Luke 8:5-8 aloud to the group.
2. **This story Jesus told is a parable. It has a hidden meaning. What do you think it means?** Encourage suggestions.

   It's about us and what happens when we hear about God. We are the ground in the story and the seed is the message about God. What happens when we hear God's message? Listen to how Jesus explained it and ask yourself which type of ground you are.
3. Choose another volunteer to read Luke 8:11-15.
4. Distribute the scrap white paper, PVA glue and paintbrushes. Tear up strips of the white paper and stick them against the cup using PVA glue, building up layers. It is not necessary to wait for each layer to dry but it is important to create even layers so that the cups will stand upright without tilting or wobbling.
5. Distribute the paints. Show the children how to mix a few drops of glue with the paint and decorate their flower pots. This will give a shiny finish when dry.
6. Display the message and invite the children to say it aloud.

   We grow in faith by staying close to God and trying to please him. Reading the Bible and praying help us to achieve this.

   You could talk about and show Scripture Union Bible reading notes for children, available from your local Scripture Union office or online at
   - scriptureunion.org.au
   - scriptureunion.org.nz
   - scriptureunion.org.uk
7. Display the words of the prayer and invite everyone to read it aloud together.

Prayer

Dear God, please help us to grow in faith by following your teaching. Amen.

The pots can take several days at a warm temperature to dry. When they are dry, fill them with potting mix and plant with seeds. Remind the children to water them regularly and place in a sunny position.

19

This novelty bookmark will be useful for Bible study or marking special passages.

Bible reading

Hebrews 4:12 *What God has said isn't only alive and active! It is sharper than any double-edged sword. His word can cut through our spirits and souls and through our joints and marrow, until it discovers the desires and thoughts of our hearts.*

You will need

- coloured card
- coloured marker pens
- scissors
- paper and pens

Time required

15 to 20 minutes

Message

God's Word is alive and active, sharper than any double-edged sword.

Faith Shapers

With your group

1. Read the Bible verse to the children. Ask if anyone has a favourite Bible passage or verse that they would like to share with the group.

2. **The Bible helps us to strengthen our connection with God.**

   The Bible is God's guidebook for life and tells us how to find true happiness.

   When we are troubled or have problems, we can find guidance in the Bible.

   It outlines God's purpose and plans for us and tells us how to please God.

   We can get to know God by reading the Bible and this will bring us closer to him.

3. Give out the pens and then take one piece of paper and write the words 'God's Word at the top of the page. Read the message once, telling people beforehand that they will need to remember it. Pass the paper around the group, asking each person to add a word to make the message. If you have a large group, start off several pieces of paper at different points around the circle so that everyone has a turn. Encourage those watching to help the person writing to think of the correct word.

4. Give out the coloured card, scissors, coloured markers, and copies of the templates.

   The children can use one of the templates provided or they may prefer to design their own bookmark.

   They could write on one side of the bookmark, 'my favourite Bible verse is' and copy the verse.

Mark my words

QUICK CRAFT – 20 minutes or less

5. Encourage the children to become familiar with the Bible by reading it daily.

   Discuss ways they could encourage each other to read it.

   If they have their Bibles with them, they should put their bookmark in an easy to read section so they know where to start.

   It can help to have a Bible reading guide. We recommend *Snapshots* and *Hotshots* for 8 to 10s and *One Up* for 11 to 14s as good guides for young people.

   They are available from Scripture Union.
   - www.scriptureunion.org.au
   - www.scriptureunion.org.nz
   - www.scriptureunion.org.uk

5. Conclude with prayer.

Prayer

Living God, thank you for giving us your Word, as a guide for our daily lives. Help us to read it often and encourage each other to do the same. Amen.

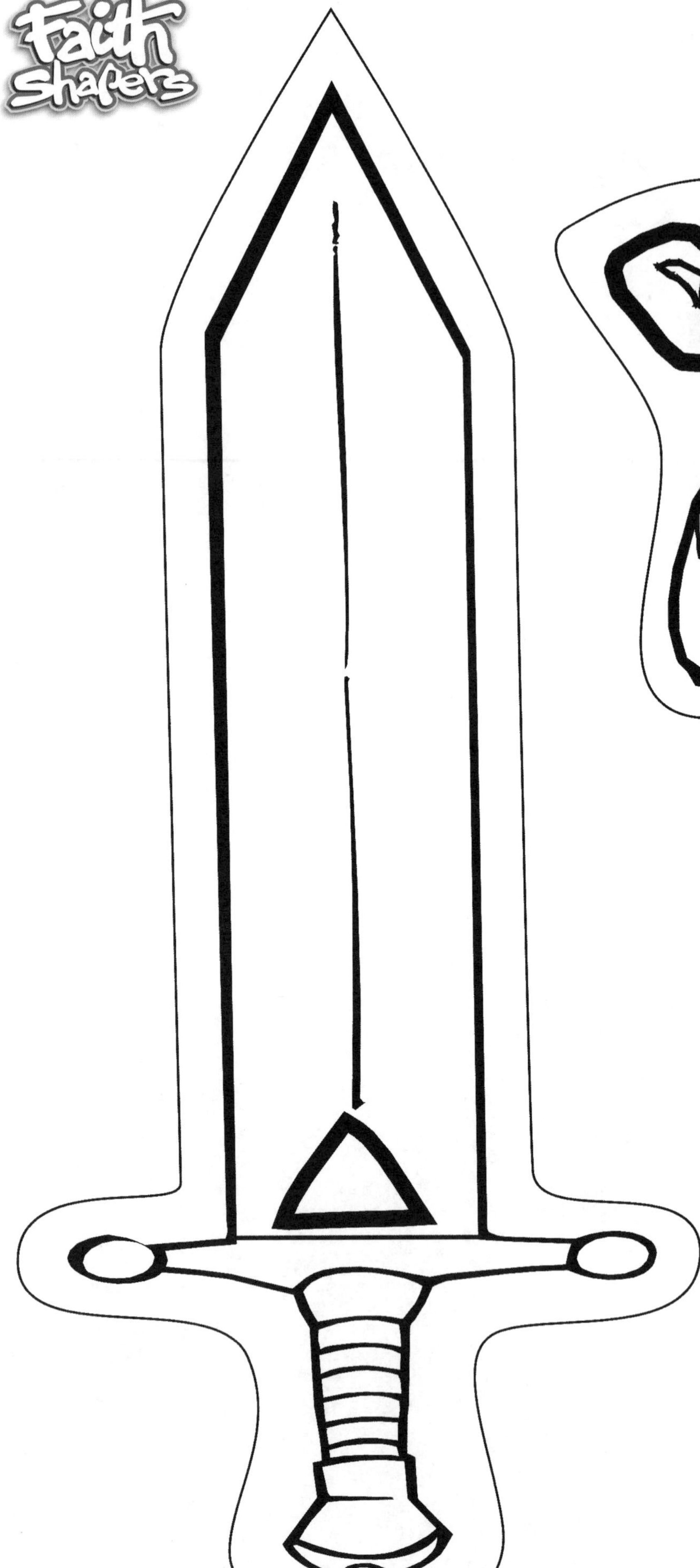

Managing behaviour IN KIDS' GROUPS

Many behaviour problems will be avoided if your programme captivates the children. Plan well to make sure each child has something appealing that they can be involved in at every moment. However, instances may still arise where the following tips will be helpful.

1. Be consistent
Consistency is a key word in behaviour management. In all that we do and say we need to show that we are dependable and that we mean what we say. We represent the God we are talking about who is the same today, yesterday and forever. God is consistent!

2. Set boundaries
Set boundaries and establish them. A positive way to encourage a child to understand your expectations quickly is to ask them which rule or expectation they are not observing. Limits help to make children feel secure. They know what is expected of them and it defines what is acceptable or otherwise. Chaos is not creative. If we do not set rules that are fair and just, then it is at our own peril.

3. Communicate clearly
Ensure that you are clearly understood. Often as we relay instructions to children we give too much information too fast. If our terminology is too advanced, too abstract or not age appropriate we are at risk of losing their attention.

4. Teach children, not lessons
Learner-based classrooms rarely see children unengaged in any subject. Evaluate your programme and ensure that it meets the learning styles of all the children. Today's child does not respond well to audible learning as the main method, so be intentional about the variety of ways in which you can relay your message.

5. Separate inappropriate behaviour from the identity of the child
Children need to hear clearly that we value them as individuals but that they may need to work on the behaviours they are presenting. It is most important that a child's sense of self worth is increased through what we do to maintain order in the group.

6. Praise freely
Praise is something we all love to receive. With a child who is off task, praising someone else for their efforts may be sufficient to bring them back on task. When this is the case, praise and positive reinforcement must be given immediately.

Praise can be given both verbally and through body language.

7. Let some things go
Ignoring some behaviours (but only those that are not escalating) can be a good strategy but only for a certain time. If the child does not come back onto task quickly, move on to giving a choice and following through.

Moving yourself to a positive position of influence can also be beneficial with children who are off task, but as soon as they are meeting your expectations give some form of positive recognition and move way. Don't fuss if it's not necessary.

8. State consequences
Giving the child a choice (or a consequence) for their actions, places the responsibility for their behaviour with them. When giving a child a choice we need to ensure that we have worked through the levels of consequences and that they are realistic. The main reason for giving a choice is to avoid misbehaviour from escalating.

9. Give them space
After giving a choice, always move away from the child and keep them in your peripheral vision. By doing this you show that you trust the child to make a good choice. However if the child's behaviour does not improve and he or she remains off task then it becomes vital that you follow through with the consequence for that choice.

Often children will test you purely to see if you will do what you said you would. Armed with that knowledge, make sure your consequence is one that you can carry out! For example, if you say that unless the inappropriate behaviour stops you will fly that person to the moon, they may find the idea quite appealing. But it is not something you are capable of executing and they will not believe you next time you give a consequence for misbehaviour.

10. Whenever you feel you need extra help recruit it!
Some children need more personal attention than others for a variety of reasons. Many times a helper can settle a child and maybe even get to know the real reason behind the presenting behaviour. In the case of the child not being able to be settled, the helper can take them away for a break and to consider their behaviour before returning. Building positive relationships is a key.

Jesus Christ cherished children and that's what we need to role model as we show them his unconditional love through our management strategies. Remember it is often the child who is hardest to love, who needs love the most!

Make this creative collage for the classroom/clubroom wall as a reminder to follow Jesus' example for living.

Bible reading

Colossians 3:12-14 *God loves you and has chosen you as his own special people. So be gentle, kind, humble, meek, and patient. Put up with each other, and forgive anyone who does you wrong, just as Christ has forgiven you. Love is more important than anything else. It is what ties everything completely together.*

You will need

- one large sheet of card for each child
- magazine pages
- glue sticks
- scissors
- PVA glue
- paintbrushes
- stapler

Time required

45 minutes

Message

Christians try to be like Jesus and follow his example (being gentle, kind, humble, meek, patient, forgiving and loving).

With your group

1. Read the Bible verses aloud to your group or have a volunteer read them.

2. **Jesus spread a message of love, compassion, kindness, forgiveness, fairness, sincerity, and honesty. Jesus is our example. He's a perfect model for us to follow. To please God, we try to live as Jesus did.**

   Ask the children to suggest some specific ways in which they can follow Jesus' example, like

   - caring about people
   - being friends with those who are not popular
   - knowing the Bible well
   - challenging unfairness
   - being involved in church
   - spending time in prayer
   - sharing what they know of God

3. Write the message on the whiteboard and invite the children to say it aloud from memory, challenging those who are able to include the words in brackets as well.

4. Give each child a sheet of card. (Some might like to work in pairs.) Distribute the magazines, scissors and glue sticks.

5. Show how to quickly go through the magazines finding pictures and words that represent the values Jesus taught. Encourage them to cut out the pictures and glue them onto the card, until the sheet is completely covered.

6. The sheets can then be taped together on the back to create a giant poster.

All for love

Distribute the paintbrushes and PVA glue for the children to paint over the entire surface of the poster. (This gives it a shiny appearance when dry.)

6. Gather around the poster and invite the children to reflect on Jesus' qualities a few moments, perhaps thinking of the things they find most difficult to copy.

Prayer

Dear Jesus, thank you for showing us how God wants us to live. Please give us your strength and power to follow your example. Amen.

> **TIP**
>
> *Keep the children focused while they are looking through the magazines by announcing a time limit and encouraging them to fill their poster quickly.*

Make it easier!

It's quite difficult for children to understand general or abstract concepts well enough to find specific examples. It's easier for them to understand the specific and concrete. But it's a skill worth developing in them since so much of the Christian faith involves abstract concepts.

Here's one way to start them off.
Pull out of the magazines some phrases, pictures and stories that represent aspects of the general qualities mentioned.
Ask them to find the word in this session's message that they fit with best.

> *Skim through the magazines at home first and remove anything that you, or the children's parents, wouldn't want discussed in your group.*

21

Make these marzipan symbols for Easter to celebrate that Jesus has risen.

Bible reading

Colossians 1:19-20 *God himself was pleased to live fully in his Son. And God was pleased for him to make peace by sacrificing his blood on the cross, so that all beings in heaven and on earth would be brought back to God.*

You will need

- marzipan (available from supermarkets)
- cornflour
- rolling pins
- food colouring of several different colours
- paper plates to take treats home
- plastic knives
- wooden skewers
- templates from page 54

Time required

40 minutes

Message

Jesus died on the cross so that our sins could be forgiven.

With your group

1. Read aloud the Bible verses.

2. **Jesus' death on the cross was all part of God's plan to save us from sin.**

   People had sinned and sin kept them from God, so God sent his Son to earth to sacrifice his life to free us from sin. When God brought Jesus back to life forever, it showed that the plan had worked, that we could be forgiven and have eternal life.

3. Write the words of the message out of order on the whiteboard. Ask the children to put the words in the right order and say the message aloud. Don't let it go on too long. Some groups may just need to be told the first word to work out the message quickly. Others will need more clues.

4. Show the templates for making the Easter marzipan shapes. They could also make small marzipan eggs.

   Give each child a lump of marzipan, a rolling pin and a plastic knife. Put the food colouring where everyone can reach it, and also a bowl of cornflour, to stop the marzipan from sticking. Supervise the children when they use the food colouring as they will only need a few drops at a time. Show them how to roll out the marzipan to 1 cm thickness and then cut out the shapes from the templates. Use a wooden skewer to draw in details.

   Lift the shapes carefully onto paper plates and cover to take home.

6. Conclude by choosing a volunteer to read the prayer.

Easter treats

Prayer

Almighty God in heaven, thank you for sacrificing your Son, Jesus, so that our sins can be forgiven. Amen.

Make it different

Make Easter vanilla cream shapes.

- 500g icing sugar
- 2 egg whites
- vanilla essence

Sift the icing sugar. Beat the egg whites and gradually stir in the icing sugar. Add a few drops of vanilla essence. Mix until smooth. Wrap in baking paper and store in an airtight container at room temperature. It can be coloured, rolled out and cut in the same way as marzipan, and hardens in about two hours. This quantity makes about fifteen symbols.

Note: This mixture is more difficult to work with than bought marzipan and hands will need to be kept coated with icing sugar.

IMPORTANT

Use a clean surface to roll out the marzipan and ensure that the children's hands and all utensils are freshly washed.

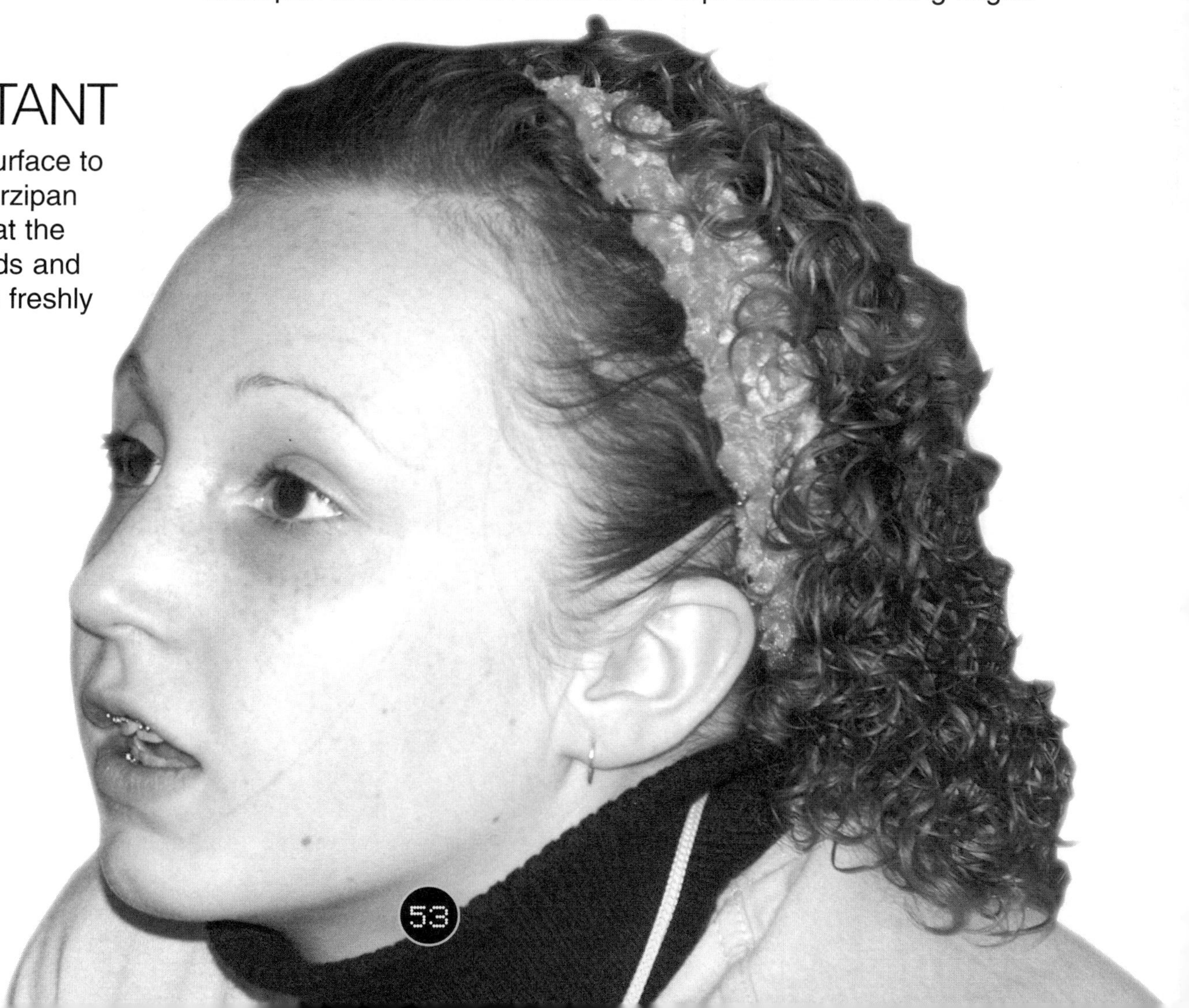

Bible verse GAMES

Mouse and Cheese (Good for short Bible verses)

On a white board or large sheet of paper draw a mouse at the base of a set of steps and a block of cheese on the top step.

Put a dash to represent each letter in the Bible verse that you want the children to discover.

Choose a child to guess a letter of the alphabet that they think may be in the verse. If that letter is in the verse, put it in place of the appropriate dash or dashes. If the letter is not in the verse make a line to show that the mouse has climbed a step and is one step closer to the cheese. Choose a different child to guess another letter and do the same again. Continue either until the mouse has reached the cheese or the verse is revealed.

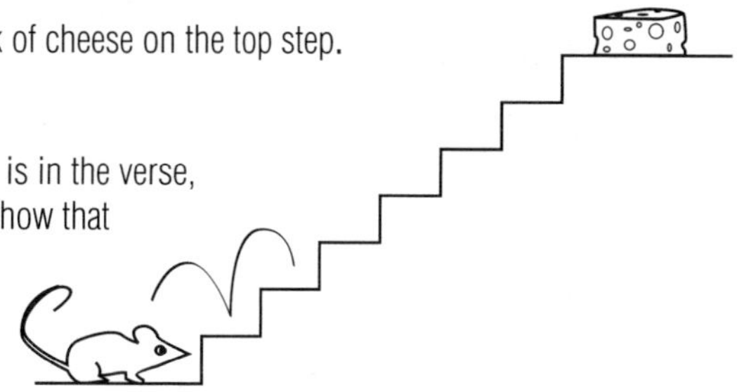

Balloon Burst (Good for lots of noise and action)

Write the words of the Bible verse on separate pieces of paper and insert each in a balloon. If you have a small group put several consecutive words on each paper. The aim is to burst the balloons, find the words and put them in order to make the Bible verse. Choose a way of bursting that fits your group such as

- Each gets a balloon and the has to burst it as quickly as possible by sitting on it.
- Ask a series of questions and the one who answers correctly gets a balloon to burst.
- Tie a balloon to the left leg of each person. Everyone runs around trying to burst others' balloons by stamping on them while trying to save their own from being burst.

Reading a Round

Write the words of the verse on separate pieces of paper and number each word according to its place in the verse. Give out the papers and on a given cue get each person to read their word in order. When the last has been read, do the same again two or three times, going back to the beginning without stopping at the end of the verse. Aim to get faster each time.

With less confident children it's easier to sit or stand, in order, in a circle.

Try these variations:

- Each person increases the volume as the verse progresses.
- Each person jumps up as they read their word.
- Each person jumps up, shouts their word and runs to a given point and back while the reading continues. (Total chaos but lots of fun, particularly for kids who find memory verses easy! Challenge them before you start to see if they can hear and memorise the whole verse as they run. When everyone is seated again let them get into small groups and pool what they remember then display the words and say it together)
- Hand out the papers so that people are not near the person whose word comes before theirs. As each word is said the speaker runs to the front and holds it so everyone can see. By the end, the words are held in order in a line at the front.
- See if you can sing up or down the scale with each new word.
- Pin the words to the back of people's shirts. Start with a line of people facing the rest of the group. Have them turn around one at a time for the group to read the word.

Encourage everyone to say the words together as they get to know the verse. However you do it, keep it fast moving and fun.

22

Making these bandannas is a great way for children to learn about being united with God through Jesus.

Bible reading

Galatians 3:26-29 *All of you are God's children because of your faith in Christ Jesus. And when you were baptised, it was as though you had put on Christ in the same way you put on new clothes. Faith in Christ Jesus is what makes each of you equal with each other, whether you are a Jew or a Greek, a slave or a free person, a man or a woman. So if you belong to Christ, you are now part of Abraham's family, and you will be given what God has promised.*

You will need

- one hemmed calico square measuring 60 cm by 60 cm for each child
- T-shirt markers (available from large chain stores in packs of ten colours)
- paper and pens

Time required

40 minutes

Message

It pleases God that we meet together to celebrate Jesus and learn more about him.

With your group

1. Read the Bible passage aloud to the children.
2. **Our faith becomes stronger as we meet to learn about God. This 'togetherness' is part of being in God's family through our belief in Jesus.**
3. Say the message aloud, then repeat it and invite the children to say it with you.
4. Distribute the pens and paper to design a bandanna logo that will show unity with the group and with God. They might like to discuss and plan their designs together.

   They could draw small crosses, hearts with 'Jesus' written in the centre, angels, the Lord's Prayer, or perhaps a Bible verse.

   Some might prefer a slogan, such as, 'God Rules' or 'JC4ME'.

   Allow about twenty minutes for this stage of the activity.
5. When the children are happy with their designs on paper, they can transfer them onto fabric. Give each child a fabric square and distribute the T-shirt markers. Warn the children to keep the markers away from their clothes.
6. When everyone has completed their bandanna, show them how to put it on. They might like to wear it to the group each week.
7. Conclude by reading the prayer.

Head on

Prayer

Our Father in heaven, we come together through Jesus Christ. Help us to value and appreciate each other so that our group is a caring group. Help us to help each other grow in faith. Amen.

Make it different

Rather than everyone doing their own bandanna, each person, can put their personal 'signature' once on everyone else's bandanna (and their own) so everyone has a record of everyone in the group.

Developing cooperation in your group

Sometimes we assume that when a group comes together the members will automatically relate well, be supportive of each other and cooperate. In fact it's not unusual instead for conflicts to occur, for some kids to feel uncomfortable or for power struggles to spring up.

In a new group your first task is to create an environment in which each member feels they belong and are 'safe'. Play getting to know you games, look for and praise cooperative behaviour, use 'we' and 'our' a lot and talk about fun activities the group will enjoy together.

Then, as members vie for different roles within the group, choose crafts that the children can work on alone but alongside other group members as they get to know them better. Making a group display of individuals' projects at this stage can help develop group spirit.

Only later, when the group has developed some cohesion and the ability to work together, is it wise to tackle projects which require cooperation and group decision making. Such projects would be group models and friezes or dramas.

Be intentional about building and maintaining group bonds. Ask God to help you identify the stage the group is at and how you can best develop an inclusive team spirit.

23

This clay jewellery is created as a way of letting others know you have faith in God.

Bible reading

Colossians 2:6-7 *You have accepted Christ Jesus as your Lord. Now keep on following him. Plant your roots in Christ and let him be the foundation for your life. Be strong in your faith, just as you were taught. And be grateful.*

You will need

- air-drying clay
- white shirring elastic
- hat elastic
- wooden skewers
- acrylic paints
- PVA glue
- paintbrushes (small and fine-tipped)
- scissors

Time required

45 minutes

Message

Christians talk about God and share their faith with others.

With your group

1. Read the Bible verses to the children.

2. **In some countries Christians meet in secret and keep their beliefs hidden from the authorities. Those who don't, sometimes end up in prison. They need to be careful about showing that they have faith. We don't have to be careful like that.**

   How can we show our faith to others? Accept answers.

3. Say the message aloud and encourage the children to say it. Invite discussion.

   Emphasise the importance of expressing our continuing faith in God through prayer, reading the Bible, attending church and Kids' Club.

   Some people choose to wear a cross or symbolic bracelet as a sign of their faith.

4. Distribute a small amount of air-drying clay to each child (a piece the size of a golf ball is sufficient). Show them how to break off small pieces and roll them into round beads. Hand out the skewers and demonstrate how to carefully push the stick through the centre of the bead to make a hole. Continue in this way until each child has made enough beads for their necklace or bracelet.

5. The next step is to give the beads a base colour with acrylic paints.

   The children should choose their own colours, and while the beads are drying, can think about what they would like to write or draw on them.

Show your faith

Some suggestions are:- 'I believe', 'God 4 Me', 'Faithful', 'God = life', or drawings of hearts, crosses or doves.

6. Distribute the fine-tipped paintbrushes for the children to decorate their beads.

   Once dry, thread the shirring elastic through the holes for the bracelets and tie a knot to secure. Use hat elastic for the necklaces.

7. Invite a volunteer to pray.

Prayer

Father God, thank you for the faith you have given us. Please help us to grow in faith and share with others what we're discovering about you.
Amen.

Note
The clay jewellery will take 24 hours to dry at room temperature.

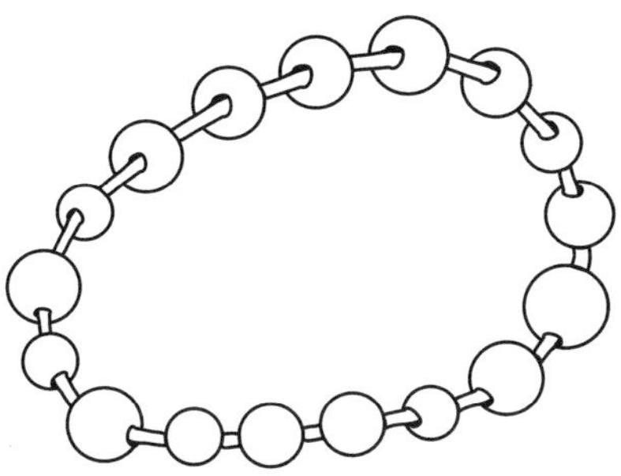

The family dimension

Every child is part of a network of relationships that we most commonly refer to as 'family'. 'Family' means different things to different people. It is important to get to know your children and their network of relationships and to do your best to establish positive relationships with them.

Communicate clearly and regularly with families about your programme.

Draw on the skill base of family members when planning activities.

Provide opportunities for family members to participate in the activities when appropriate and include all-age activities to which family members are invited.

Foster provision of programmes which provide parenting and relational skills and promote them through your group.

Recruit mature people to informally chat with parents and carers before and after your programme.

24

Children can chat about God's message as they make this fabric bag to keep their Bible in.

Bible reading

2 Timothy 3:15-17 *Since childhood, you have known the Holy Scriptures that are able to make you wise enough to have faith in Christ Jesus and be saved. Everything in the Scriptures is God's Word. All of it is useful for teaching and helping people and for correcting them and showing them how to live. The Scriptures train God's servants to do all kinds of good deeds.*

> ***IMPORTANT***
>
> *Send a note home with the children the week before this activity reminding them to bring their Bibles.*

You will need

- one piece of felt or fabric 70 cm by 30 cm for each child (trim edges with pinking scissors to prevent fraying)
- craft glue
- pins
- scissors
- felt or other non-fraying fabric scraps (assorted colours) to decorate
- self-adhesive Velcro (one 10 cm strip for each child)
- needles and sewing thread (optional)
- paper and pens

> *When choosing fabric look for what will appeal to the children. Denim, funky fur, vinyl and cute patterns are usually popular.*

Time required

45 minutes

Message

The Bible makes us wise enough to be saved and can help us and others to live well. (This message is optional. See instruction 3.)

With your group

1. Read the Bible passage aloud asking the group to listen out for at least three things it says about the Scriptures. Share what they heard.

2. **It is vital to study and learn from the Bible to understand God's message. The Bible shows us how to live. There are stories that give us clues about wise ways of living and ways that lead to disaster. Some passages give commands and others give wise advice. The Bible records the life of Jesus who is the best example to follow.**

3. Use the message listed here or write the Bible verses on the whiteboard and ask the groups to make up a message in five minutes. Invite the groups to share their message and vote for the one that best reflects the Bible verses.

4. Hand out the fabric for the Bible bags. Show them how to fold the piece in half right sides facing outward. Align the edges, and carefully glue the side edges together, leaving the top edge open. Pin the glued edges together. The seams can be oversewn with thick coloured thread (optional).

Best seller

5. Using the fabric scraps, the children can decorate their Bible bags. The bags should be individual and personal to each child, just as their relationship with God is. They could include their name or initials cut out and glued on the front and designs such as animals, flowers, abstract shapes, smiley faces, hearts, stars and clouds.

6. To finish the Bible bags, attach the self-adhesive Velcro strips to the top of the inside edges. The pins can be removed from the side edges once the glue has dried. The bags should not be used until the glue is completely dry.

7. Encourage the children to find time to read their Bible every day. Conclude by choosing a volunteer to read the prayer.

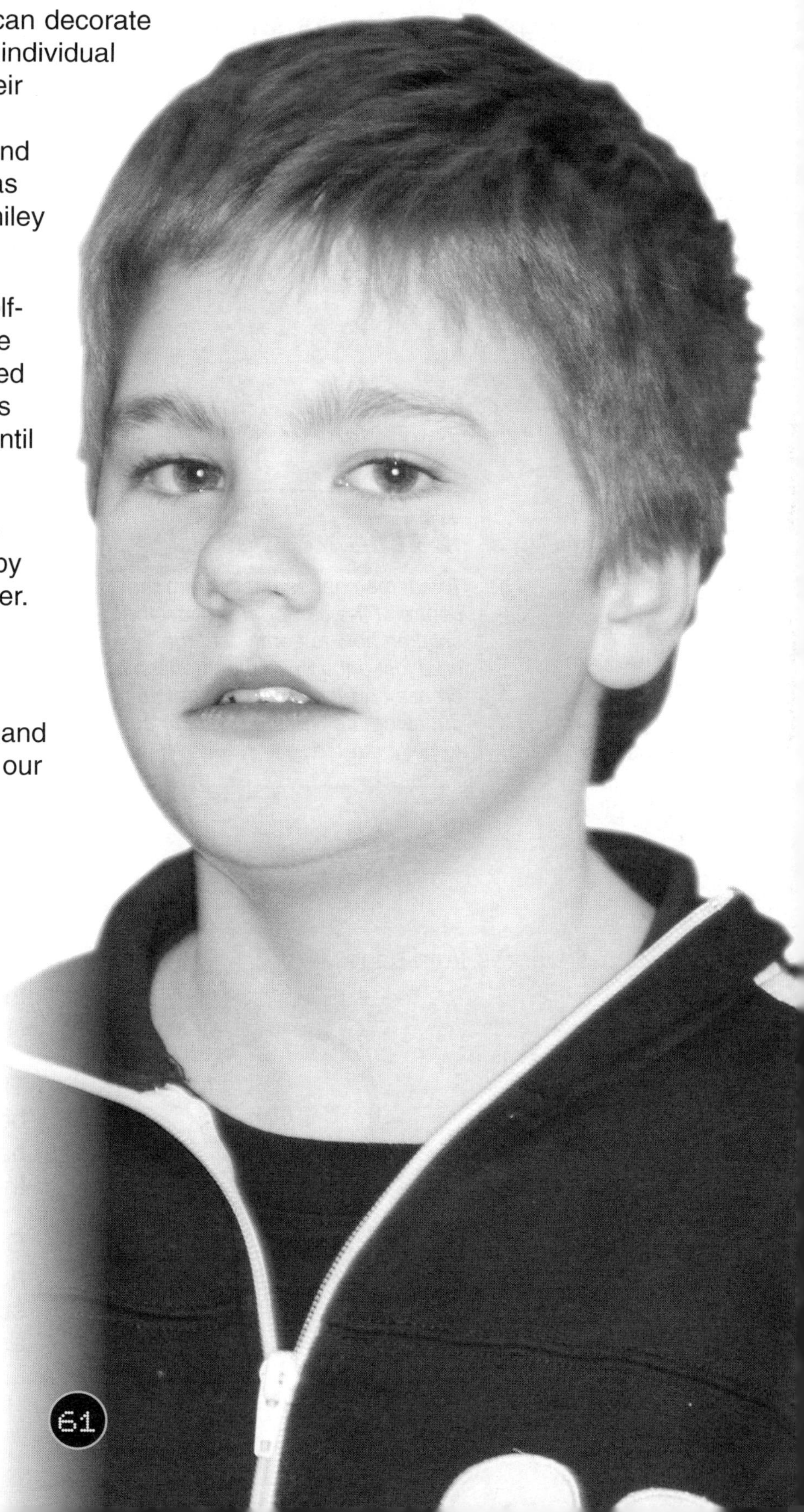

Prayer

Almighty God, help us to hear your voice and understand your message when we read our Bibles. Amen.

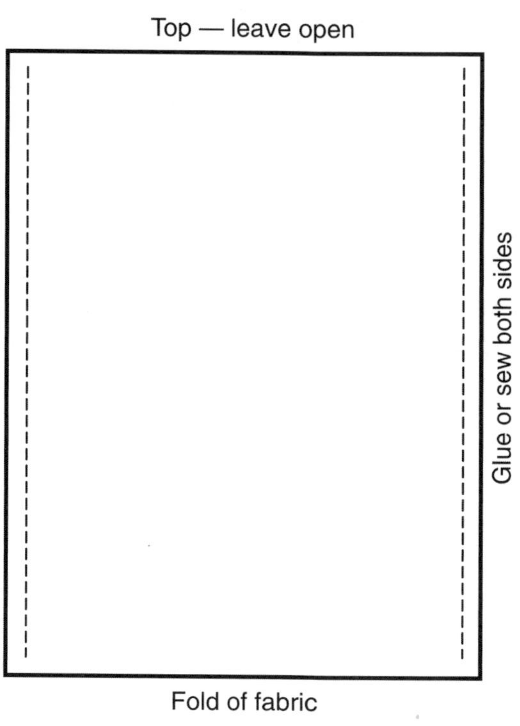

This stained glass window is an effective reminder that God is the light in our lives.

Bible reading

Psalms 119:105 *Your word is a lamp that gives light wherever I walk.*

You will need

- one sheet of black card 30 cm by 22 cm for each child
- cellophane, assorted colours including yellow
- scissors
- PVA glue (dries clear)
- white chalk
- prepared stencils from page 64.

> **TIP**
>
> *To cut the shapes neatly from the centre of the cardboard, show the children how to gently fold the card just enough so that it doesn't crease and then make a straight cut along the line they want to cut, to get it started.*

Time required

30 minutes

Message

God's teachings in the Bible are a good guide for life.

With your group

1. Before the children arrive, write the message on the whiteboard. Choose a volunteer to read the Bible verse aloud to the group.

2. **One reason God gave us his Word, the Bible, is so that we can discover how to deal with our problems and worries and make wise choices in life.**

   God also wants us to pray to him and ask him to guide us and show us what to do.

   The Bible is reliable, but it's not much good to us if we don't read it or find out what it says. Reading a little every day will help us to know God better and keep us close to him.

3. Read aloud the message, then invite the children to say it with you.

4. Give each child a sheet of black card and two pieces of coloured cellophane. Distribute the scissors, white chalk and glue.

5. Show the children how to place the stencil on the black card and use the chalk to draw the outline. Then cut out the shapes from the card and discard, leaving the candle shape in the card.

   The children can also cut a decorative border or pattern if they wish. When they have finished, the cellophane is glued onto the card.

6. Once dry, the decorations can be taken home, or placed against the windows, in a sunny position. Conclude with the prayer around the theme of God's light.

Guiding light

Prayer

Dear God, help us to follow your light,
as you guide us through life.
Amen.

Children's leaders are stars!

The essence of ministering among children is a relationship of genuine love and concern for the children, out of which will grow faith and trust. It's more than programs and teaching. It is more about being than doing.

There will be tough times but remember you do not stand alone.

Take advantage of training opportunities as they come your way.

Enjoy time with other leaders of children.

Spend time in prayer.

Trust in our faithful God.

' … you shine like stars in the universe as you hold out the word of life.'
Philippians 2:15,16

Fold along line and cut
out the shaded sections
to make a stencil.

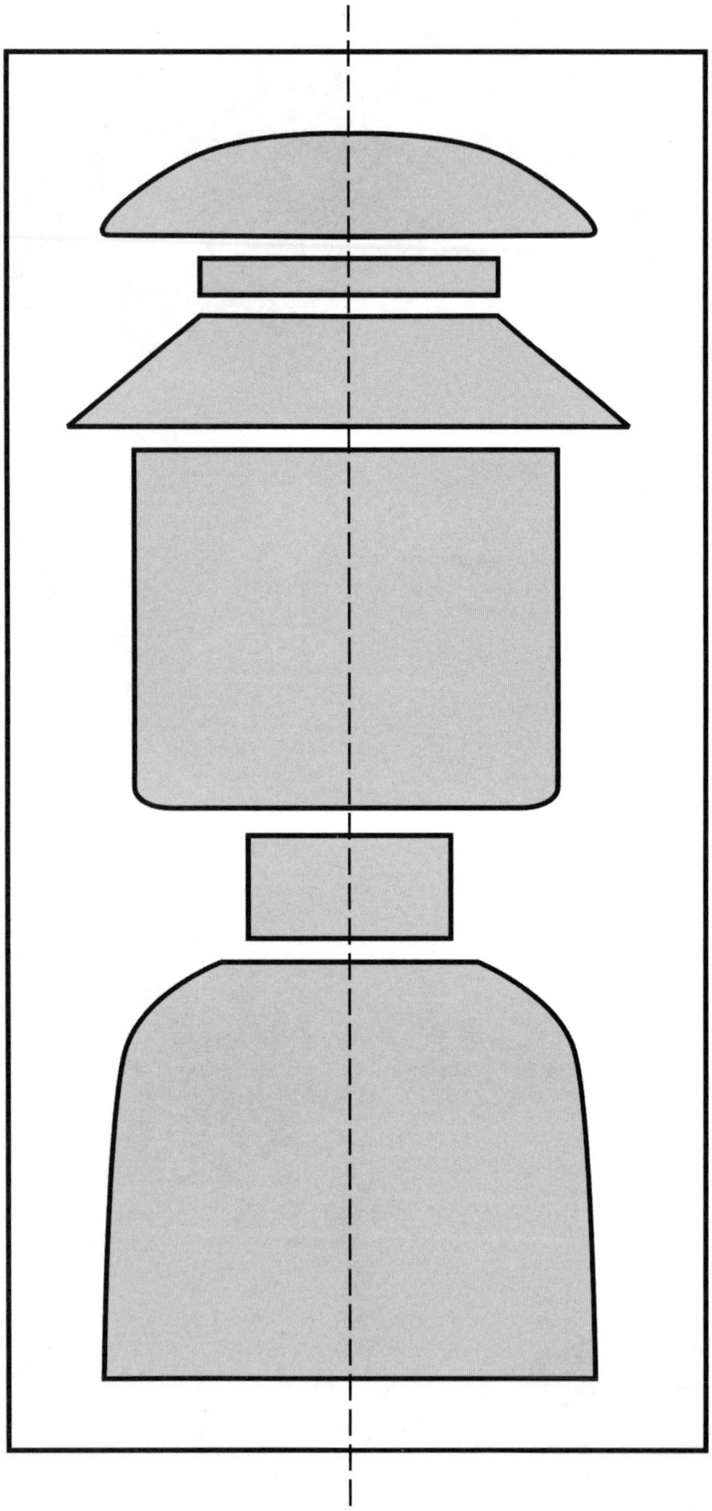

Fold along line and cut
out the shaded sections
to make a stencil.

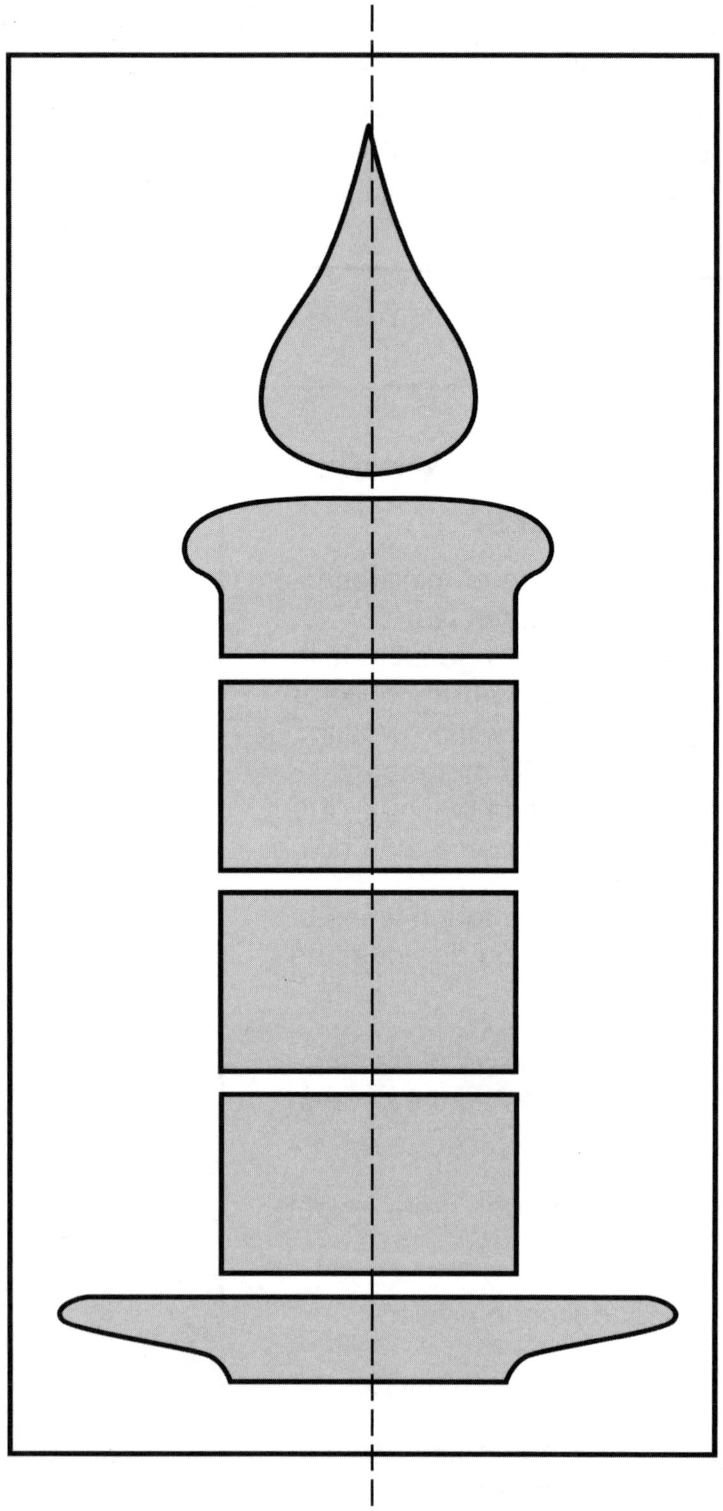